ANGLING

the

WORLD

ANGLING
the
WORLD

TEN SPECTACULAR ADVENTURES IN FLY FISHING

ROY TANAMI

THE LYONS PRESS
Guilford, Connecticut

An imprint of The Globe Pequot Press

For my parents, Ken and Seiko Tanami.

~

The Lyons Press is an imprint of The Globe Pequot Press.

Text design by Sheryl P. Kober

All photos by Roy Tanami unless otherwise noted.

Library of Congress Cataloging-in-Publication Data

Tanami, Roy.
Angling the world : ten spectacular adventures in fly fishing / Roy Tanami.
p. cm.
ISBN 978-1-59921-394-1
1. Fly fishing--Anecdotes. 2. Tanami, Roy. I. Title.
SH456.T346 2008
799.12'4--dc22
2008024496

Printed in China

10 9 8 7 6 5 4 3 2 1

CONTENTS

ACKNOWLEDGMENTS

Huge thanks to the following folks for their friendship, support, and vital contributions not only to this book, but also to enriching my life both in and out of fly fishing. A huge apology to all those who have also looked after, supported, and otherwise aided, tolerated, and/or bailed me out along the way that I've forgotten or otherwise neglected to mention here—you know who you are. Looking forward to our next grand adventure together sometime soon.

Joe Daniel, editor and publisher of *Wild On The Fly* literary magazine, and Perry Bergman, art director of same. Tim Romano (*Angling Trade* magazine/F&S Flytalk blog). Vern Olson. Hannah and Alice Belford (Damdochax River Lodge). KC Walsh (Simms). Christer Sjoberg (Loop). Peter Morrison and Marc Bale (Sage). Andy Murray (Hardy). Juan Luis Ariztegui "Juancho." David Watts. Geoff Straight (Bell II Lodge). Dan Vermillion (Sweetwater Travel). Alejandro Menendez (Ea. Maria Behety). Alejandro DiTomasso (Ea. Guer Aike/Carlotta). Octavio Salles and Mane Figuera (Amazon Fly Fishing). John and Robbin Gemmel (Riverview Lodge). Avalons Fishing (Cuba). Cinco Rios Lodge (Chile). Martin Knustson. Luke and Mary Coady. Peter and Martina Kapolak. Mike O'Connor. Jim Nudelman. Paul Swacina. Ed Ward. Pete Soverel. Dave and Nancy Mitchell. Tom and Betsy Murray. Mario Zwetzig. Alberto Zwetzig "Chu Chu." Albert Zwetzig. Claudio Martin. Diego Coscia "Pollo." Jim Allen (Kispiox Fishing Company/Bearclaw Lodge). Viviana Costilla. Fernando Mosso. Juan Dumas. Frank Amato. Lisa Winbourne. Mike Osterman. Rich Jorgenson. Deke Welles. Don Woods. Parker Jefferson. Hans Sawatsky. Terry Donovan. Dave Hall. Al Belheumer. Vaile Long. Devon Young. Robert Mackwood (Seventh Avenue Literary Agency). Jeff Serena. Jane Sheppard. Scott Bowen.

Opposite page:
Rio Gallegos, Argentina

FOREWORD

As the editor of *Wild On The Fly*, a literary fly-fishing travel magazine, I have found that the rarest and most valuable skill set in outdoor journalism is the ability of a single person to both write well *and* take great photographs. But good luck in discovering someone with that gift. He is as exceptional as a wild ten-pound trout on a dry fly.

To be honest, just finding a genuine travel wordsmith in today's world of Chatwin, Cahill, and Krakauer wannabes is a big enough challenge. It seems everyone who ever went on an exotic fishing trip fancies himself the next Joe Brooks, only without any of the attendant vision, writing ability, or sometimes even remedial understanding of his own spoken language. Perhaps the rich experience of fly fishing does that to people, liberating their need to tell others of how they were touched. But for most aspiring authors, it is a muse best kept tethered to the confines of the personal journal. Going public demands a level of literary acumen that, frankly, most folks just don't have—although that certainly doesn't seem to stop anyone. The cavalcade of unsolicited manuscripts and story proposals that crosses my desk is often mind-boggling in both measure and mediocrity.

But finding a good photographer is, in my opinion, even more difficult. As with great writing, great photography often borders on art. The rudiments of both can be learned, but which is more innate, voice or vision? I would suggest vision. With hard work and discipline, a writer can be fledged, perhaps even created from scratch, but the best photographers are simply born. A writer's voice is crafted, evolving with experience and often changing over the long course of life. A good photographer's vision, however, seems hardwired from the start. Stimulate it with the technical tools of picture making and the visual raw material of life, and magic ensues.

Yet, for one of these disciplines, the times they are a changing. The inviolability of good writing is preserved by its own process—there is still no such thing as a point-and-write pen. And, while laptop computers

Opposite page:
Rio Grande, Tierra del Fuego, Argentina

ix

and word processing programs have made the manual typewriter and even handwriting in general obsolete and allow for endless and painless editing (which is a good thing), you still have to find the right words and put them down in an order that tells truth and inspires reaction. There is no technology out there that makes the creative part any easier.

But photography, on the other hand, has endured a paradigm change in the form of point-and-shoot digital cameras, which, frankly, have stolen the stage from professional shooters. The oft-repeated complaint from those in the visual arts that "everyone is a photographer" has an element of truth. Cynics claim that film is dead, and with it much of the technical craft of photography. The digital revolution has made it possible for almost anyone to shoot a decent photograph, which, in the publishing industry, has resulted in a plethora of "usable" images. I don't suggest that this supplants great photography—in fact in some ways, quite the opposite. But it *has* raised the bar for what constitutes a great, or at least original, image and, hence, has made finding the image-maker only that much harder.

So when an individual as talented as Roy Tanami enters your world, as he did mine shortly after the turn of the millennium, you sit up and take notice. Here was a guy who was not only an extremely talented photographer by trade, but also a surprisingly eloquent (for a lensman!) writer on the side. Roy still makes no claims as a scribe, preferring to exploit only his shooting abilities, but I think he's wrong. His photographs are excellent and at times even breathtaking, but his true faculty lies in his unique literary hash of keen observation, strong wit, and—I don't know how else to say it—Canadian irony. He is a consummate storyteller, as you will soon discover, and while it is always an overindulgence of eye-candy editing one of his photographic shoots, it is the first read of a Tanami manuscript that I look forward to the most.

When I first met Roy, the idea for *Wild On The Fly* was simply an improbable scheme percolating away on a back burner while I worked a "real" job researching content for an early Priceline-like outdoor-travel Web site called *Adventure Deal.* My role was to find fly-fishing outfitters wishing to sell their trips online, and inquiries led me to Roy's Arctic Heli-Fishing operation, which he was then running high above the Arctic Circle. The genuine thing about Roy as an angling photojournalist is that he truly walks the talk. At barely five foot four but built like Genghis Khan, he is a passionate and practiced fisherman with years of guiding and wilderness outfitting experience.

We hit it off instantly on the phone, and long conversations followed where we discovered each other's true proclivity for journaling about angling. When the dot-com bubble burst and *Adventure Deal* disappeared faster than a bad bet, we just kept talking. Soon it was decided that a story on Arctic Heli-Fishing for giant sea-run Arctic char would be a perfect feature for the inaugural issue of *Wild On The Fly,* and so it was.

That was over five years ago, and in that time Roy has written and photographed ten major features for the magazine that have taken him to Kamchatka, Russia, for steelhead; Brazil for peacock bass; Cuba for bonefish, tarpon, and permit; Northern British Columbia for steelhead; Argentina for trout, doves, and wine; Mongolia for taimen; Argentina for sea-run browns and Atlantic-run steelhead; and New Zealand for "mouse trout." He has also co-produced *Wild On The Fly* video productions in many of the above locations, as well as in the Seychelles for milkfish, giant trevally, and triggerfish; in Chile for trout; in Argentina for freshwater dorado; and in Costa Rica for sailfish.

All of this searching for wild fish in wild waters has resulted in the remarkable collection of stories you now hold in your hand. Savor it as you would a premium Russian vodka, an aged Cuban rum, or a rich Argentine Malbec. For it is from an ever-expanding cultural stew of fishing, friends, food, and frivolity that Roy's stories emerge. Together they are your passport to a world of extraordinary angling adventure. But be warned: This is a journey one must not take lightly, as the unabashed nature of Roy's own awe and wonderment, enthusiasm, and reflection is dangerously contagious and will likely lead you astray. Proceed with caution!

—Joseph E. Daniel
Boulder, Colorado

Opposite page:
Eg/Urr River, Huvsgul Province, Mongolia

INTRODUCTION

More often than not these days, I find, sprinkled like jewels in the sea of spam and other unavoidable annoyances in my inbox, fabulous photographs of fish. Some are sent to me from local sources, and, as I am a native British Columbian, this usually means images of large, bright, beefy wild steelhead. The others, though, often come from the far-flung corners of the globe, and it's almost impossible to predict what they might be.

On any given day, it could be Mike holding a hefty twelve-pound bone from the fly-fishing Disneyland that is the Florida Keys. Or it could be Vern from that same flats paradise, most likely with a massive tarpon or even a permit. Then again, it might be Dave or Nancy with a spectacular sailfish, marlin, or dorado just caught in the surreal blue-water zone of Pacific Costa Rica, or even Octavio or Mane with the latest, wildest, craziest-colored pig of a peacock bass that fell for a fly in some deep, dark corner of the Brazilian Amazon. Quite often, these digital treasures are sent by *mis hermanos* Argentinos: from Fernando, Mario, Albert, Pollo, or Claudio, reminding me of the scintillatingly beautiful rainbows consistently found in the breathtakingly wild and scenic streams twisting deep within the jagged peaks of the Andes. From this crowd, though, the images could be of anything, from the gilded, toothy, freshwater dorado found in the steamy marshes of northern Argentina, to the massive, silver-bullet sea trout of wild and wind-

Opposite page:
Rio Gallegos, Argentina

Opposite page:
Boat repair, Rio Negro,
Amazonas Province, Brazil

swept southern Patagonia, right through to the mysterious, feisty, and mirror-bright Atlantic steelhead found nowhere else in the world but the chalky-blue, glacial currents of the Rio Santa Cruz.

Whatever the case, from north to south, east to west, at any given time, somewhere in the world something is in season, and based on the contents of my e-mail messages, it's starting to seem like whatever it is and wherever it swims, someone I know is out there throwing a fly at it. As a fly fisherman, I find this notion in itself quite a beautiful thing to ponder. It's the allure and promise of an endless summer; the delight in knowing a close friend could be out fulfilling his or her passion at any given moment, and, of course, the purely selfish pleasure of imagining myself right there alongside him or her doing exactly the same thing. But above and beyond the countless hours of high-quality daydreaming fueled by these photos, more and more I think the truly fascinating state of affairs my inbox reflects is what fly fishing has become today.

Our sport is now conducted on a truly global scale. Previously prohibitive boundaries of geography, technological limitations of fishing gear and clothing, and even preconceived notions of what a "fly-fishing species" is, essentially no longer exist or are rapidly falling by the wayside. Indeed, our venerable low-tech pastime of flicking feathers at fish, like most other human pursuits, has gone space-age and digital, and like no other time in history, the world really is our oyster.

We live in an age where, given twenty-four hours or so, it's possible to travel to just about any point on the face of the earth with relative ease, and once there, to transmit a digital image to just about anywhere else in about 2.4 seconds. Sure, travel can be a bit pricey at times, especially in reaching the truly remote and exotic locales, but despite this annoying detail, the fact of the matter is it can be done, and, increasingly, fly fishers are doing it.

From what I can only attribute to ethereal factors like good karma, blind luck, and questionable decision making, rather than to steely, focused ambition, over the past several years I've become one of those fly fishers, somehow ending up on a whirlwind ride though this brave new world of fly fishing. Consistently and absolutely ignoring the wisdom that says you should never make your hobby your career, I've literally crisscrossed the globe, making a living as camp grunt, fishing guide, lodge operator, and fishing photojournalist or filmmaker, following a checkered life and career path winding ever deeper into this fantastic and ever broadening world of contemporary fly fishing. As any fly fisher knows, if you're not careful, the sport will take over all aspects of your life—professional, personal, and otherwise—and I guess I never was very good at being careful.

As an angler, though, it's a life I couldn't have dreamed up even in my wildest moments. Wandering the globe to fish is every bit as good as it sounds, and the outrageous fishing is just a part of it. All of fly fishing's considerably powerful seduction—the quest for adventure and discovery; meeting new challenges, people, and environments; and the pleasures of being in direct contact with the elemental, pristine, and most beautiful aspects of nature—often seem amplified in the extreme and exotic edges of this world. In terms of career, the picture is not quite as rosy. For as good as the job description may appear, the job itself lacks the standard perks most careers are supposed to provide, such as opportunity for financial gain, a basis for domestic and social stability, a retirement fund, and a basic level of societal acceptance. Ignoring wisdom, it seems, always comes at a price.

The articles here were originally published in *Wild On The Fly* literary magazine. As a group, they have no particular focus or organization, except that most are about places I wanted to go and somehow managed to garner the assignments to cover. As such, they are not intended to represent an All-time Top Ten Fly-Fishing Destinations list that marketing executives seem so fond of today. In fact, since I haven't covered an Atlantic salmon story (not yet anyway), this present collection wouldn't even make my personal top ten. These articles do, however, cover many of the well-known dream destinations and species in the world, as well as some of the truly exotic and exploratory fisheries that few people have ever experienced, right through to an off-the-charts do-it-yourself trip in southern Argentina. They

Uhtolok River Camp,
Kamchatka, Russia

Opposite page:
Perito Moreno Glacier,
Argentina

xvi

are easily *among* the top ten fly-fishing experiences in the world today, and, therefore, as a collection they may even provide a more interesting and representative glimpse of what's going on out there in the world of fly angling than one limited only to destination resort angling.

Along the way, in addition to reporting these specific stories, I've also had ample opportunity and cause to ruminate on what might be termed the grand and timeless themes of our sport—the questions that have occupied the minds of fly anglers through the ages and that resonate with both home-water anglers as well as those compelled to travel for their sport. Throughout its history, fly fishing has always been a cerebral exercise, as evidenced by its long and extensive literary tradition.

Periods of profound solitude, opportunities for genuine, unencumbered soul-searching, and the constant testing of ideas seem built into its very foundations. Fly fishing forces us all to ponder basic philosophical questions fairly often, even beyond those involving life and career.

The essays presented here include my small contributions to this long-running tradition of navel-gazing about fly fishing generally, but also about the thorny questions that confront today's widely wandering global angler. Just as the attractions of our sport seem more compelling and intense at the extreme edges, so do the questions. After all, watching a helicopter disappear in the distance after being dropped off alone in the harsh and uninhabited vastness of the Canadian Arctic, or enduring a mind- and butt-numbing Argentina-to-Seychelles flight with two successive twelve-hour layovers, first in New York and then in Paris, or boarding an ancient Russian helicopter bound for the Middle of Nowhere Mountains of Mongolia, all in the name of fly fishing, does tend to force a rather close examination of yourself, your choices in life and sport, and just how you ever let it get this far. My hope is that these musings will provide a conceptual context for modern global fly fishing and a thematic backdrop for the collection of articles. Admittedly, though, they could just as easily be seen as a series of rationalizations for what some might consider extreme and irresponsible behavior.

Cayo Largo, Cuba

Opposite page:
Rio Santa Cruz Valley,
Argentina

of any era. But just as access to our home waters and local fisheries increases, so it does as well for the wilder, more remote and exotic places left on earth. Luckily, we live in a time where the options in this regard are as open to us as never before. Fishing today certainly isn't what it used to be, but from my point of view, it's only getting better. I hope this book will make you feel the same way, whether your fly-fishing dreams are fulfilled on the familiar banks of a home stream or out on the very edges of the earth. Tight lines and happy trails.

WHY THE FLY?

In life and fly fishing the simplest questions often lead to more complex questions, yet rarely to truly definitive answers. Ask any good flats guide how best to attach a beefy bite tippet to a skinny class tippet, and he or she will whip you off a very complex bimini/Huffnagle knot or some equally complicated equivalent in seconds flat, and also be able to tell you in definitive detail, why. Ask that same fly angler the seemingly innocuous question of why he or she fly fishes, though, and you could be there for hours. Better yet, sit down and ask yourself this question and you may be occupied for days, or perhaps even longer.

I don't really know exactly why I came to the fly, and up until quite recently, I never really gave it much thought. But since realizing that I've allowed fly fishing, for better or for worse, to commandeer my entire

That fishing "just ain't what it used to be" is probably the most common complaint passed down through the generations. To be sure, as the world shrinks and pressure on natural resources grows, our fish, the places they live, and the quality of our experiences as fly anglers are often the first to take the hit. Indeed, the quest to find bigger and better fish has probably always been the main impetus for the traveling angler

life, personal, professional, and otherwise, for at least the past two decades, an examination of sorts was clearly in order. Especially since, among other things, this life somehow still hasn't produced the shiny new Range Rover or the driveway it should be sitting in, if you get my drift. But the more I thought about it, the more complicated and elusive the answer became. Just what is it about our sport that not only draws us in but elicits such an overwhelmingly passionate and even addictive devotion?

I was soon lost deep within this quagmire of my own creation. Many of the standard answers I came up with were common to other forms of fishing and therefore really didn't address the point at hand. Confused, confounded, and sweating a deadline, I desperately reached out for help. On the water, on the phone, and on e-mail, I sought the wisdom and opinions of trusted fly-fishing friends, clients, and mentors from the world over. I turned to Scotch and tried to channel the likes of Haig-Brown, Joe Brooks, and even old man Walton himself. But after countless hours of consideration and consternation, the only short, simple conclusion that I eventually reached was that there was in fact no truly satisfactory answer to the question of why we fly fish. Each of us who ever picked up a fly rod did so for different reasons, and as our lives as fly fishers progressed, they did so as well for an infinite variety of individual, personal reasons.

So there it was. After months of searching for the profound, I had discovered the painfully obvious.

However, not unlike fly fishing, the process in itself was its own reward, and my little journey into the psyche of the fly fisher was in many ways as fascinating as an exotic fishing trip to some faraway corner of the world. In fact, if there is now one thing more wondrously mysterious to me in the world of fishing than what possesses a fish to move to a fly and then actually eat it, it is what possesses us to throw those flies in the first place. For if nothing else, the other inescapable conclusion I reached about fly fishers is that no matter where we fish, or what we fish for, we truly are a special kind of crazy.

Take the fly itself. As much as we paralyze ourselves, both at the bench and on the water, over the minutiae of size, shape, color, and materials in our flies, we conveniently choose to ignore the fact that each and every one of them has at least one obvious, relatively large, and decidedly unnatural looking hook sticking out of it. To an observant and non-delusional individual, just this one feature alone might be enough to disqualify even the most perfectly tied fly from being considered something that might fool a fish, especially if fish were indeed as smart, selective, wily, and discerning as we often like to think they are. Somehow, though, it never seems to occur to us that it's only because we've chosen to try to catch fish in such a weird way that they ever seem intelligent to begin with. After all, how many of those skittery and seemingly impossible Keys bones have you seen suckered into swallowing a soaked shrimp? Or, those big and elusive British Columbia steelhead so

"River X," Nunavut, Canada

easily seduced by a square of nylon stocking wrapped around a big, stinking chunk of roe? And, let's not even talk about how stupid permit can be with live crabs.

But to us, *how* we catch fish is far more important than *if* we catch fish, and in fact, no matter how coveted the species, most of us would rather play golf or even go to the dentist before doing anything as ridiculously obvious as catch fish with bait. Indeed, the very idea that catching fish can be too easy (and therefore boring) not only seems central to our way of thinking, but also directly

contrary to what other types of anglers would consider the ideal. It's no small wonder, then, that at best, our bait- and hardware-fishing brethren often consider us a harmless and somewhat eccentric cult, because, after all, that's kind of what we are. Really, how else can you look upon a group of folks who not only go out of their way to make things harder on themselves, but get addicted to matching wits with fish by employing a smoke-and-mirrors show involving eclectic cocktails of fluff and feathers wound onto hooks?

Despite all this, if there's one place we all seem to take asylum, it is in the belief that our approach to fishing is somehow more "evolved," or "enlightened" than that of others. But if evolution implies progress, it seems our main advancement has been to overthink fishing to the extent that catching fish really becomes beside the point. What the primary point of fly fishing then becomes, of course, is open to infinite interpretation, and perhaps that in itself is the true beauty of our sport. But whatever the case, we've transformed the basic, almost primal activity of catching fish into something resembling a confounding, oxymoronic, Zen-like mind game: fishing where a fish in hand is not necessarily the goal. I'm sure psychiatrists have a term for this, and I'm betting that it's probably not "enlightened."

That said, perhaps the truly compelling aspect of our sport, and the main thing that sets it apart from other forms of angling, is that fly fishing is a largely cerebral exercise. A fly, after all, is an entirely human creation. It's an idea, an abstraction, and a theory in ways that bait just isn't. When a fish eats bait, there's little mystery in it—proof of nothing but the fulfillment of a basic biological function. When a fish takes a fly, though, it confirms a multitude of theoretical assumptions, as wild as they may be, that the angler has made from the time he or she tied or bought the fly to the time it was let loose on the water. And this process of validation or rejection of our ideas is one key aspect of fly fishing that I believe engages us so fully, even if our ideas are only formulated in order to try and determine what a fish might be thinking.

And perhaps it's because our ideas in this heady arena are delivered at the ends of fly casts that we place so much importance on our casting performance, as it's only natural to think that our ideas would be most persuasive when presented with as much artistry and grace as we can muster. So while the cast is the defining physical act of our sport, I like to think there is a conceptual component behind it too, over and above its inherent practical or even aesthetic value. Truly elegant casting is a skill that is as beautiful to behold as it is fulfilling to execute, demanding a commitment to proficiency that in itself is powerful and worthwhile. In fact, for many fly fishers, casting, even more than catching, is where the true pleasure in fly fishing lies. This is understandable, perhaps, for we do have to do a fair bit of casting, and just as with fly tying and selection, the opportunities for self-expression and creativity here seem limited only by the imagination of the angler.

Opposite page:
Eg/Urr River, Huvsgul Province, Mongolia

Opposite page:
South Island, New Zealand
Tim Romano

Of course the really crazy part of all this is that the final arbiters of all our elaborate, fanciful, feathery, and elegant theories happen to be fish, and this is where it can all go seriously haywire, for realistically, the fish couldn't give a wink about any of our machinations. So many great fish have been caught on the ends of the ugliest casts, with the rattiest flies, after the most horrific mends, and other such travesties (not to mention by sheer accident), and so many more have been lost simply by us prematurely ripping what we considered to be unacceptable casts out of the water, that I sometimes marvel at our commitment to the method. But again, this does reinforce the notion that in fly fishing, it's more about the process than the final result.

But there is a fly in the fly-fishing ointment, so to speak, and, somewhat ironically, it lies in the fact that we all still very much want to catch fish. And herein lies the rub between the sharper challenges we seek and the inherent limitations of our chosen approach that provide those very challenges. In other words, while we've adopted a more difficult method for its greater rewards, we react in fascinating and sometimes contradictory ways when the going gets tough. For some, the very idea that a fish can't be caught on a fly only fuels an intense obsession to find a way to do so. Yet for others, it can lead to techniques that flirt with the very edges of the sport.

The growing trend toward bobber-fishing with fly rods is the example of the latter instance that confuses me the most. In its most extreme incarnation, this technique involves big, fuzzy "strike indicators" that would be more at home in a cheerleader's hands, as well as balloons, hinged leaders, plastic beads, multiple split shot, something called a "slinky," toothpicks, and sundry other encumbrances so antithetical to fly fishing that even casting the whole circus on a fly line becomes an oxymoronic, or perhaps just simply moronic exercise. It certainly takes most of the artistry and all of the grace out of fly casting. And while there may very well be a fly at the end of it all, this is simply spin-fishing or baitcasting with a fly rod. Unquestionably, it's an effective way to catch fish. But at that point, why not just do it right and get a level-wind reel loaded with mono, a drift rod, a collection of dink floats, swivels, and pencil lead, and save fly fishing for another day?

Indeed, the most effective fly fishers I've known in the world—those anglers who seem to magically and consistently pull fish out of the most unlikely places and impossible situations when no one else can—all seem to achieve their results with patience, knowledge, confidence, observation, and, as funny as this might sound, a kind of Zen-like serenity, rather than resorting to desperate moves based on gear gimmicks. Of course, this is a manifestation of virtuosity, and it would seem that the quest to achieve this state not only promises a far more interesting journey than doing anything as tedious and awkward as chucking gear with a fly rod, but in fact represents much of what fly fishing is really all about. Most important perhaps, the most fulfilled fly fishers I

know don't even consider the body count as a part of the equation, yet ironically, they are often also among the most productive fish catchers.

Call me an old-fashioned purist, but I believe the headlong rush to fish-catching efficacy at all costs has never been a hallmark of our sport. If it were, we'd have all stayed with or switched to bait or conventional gear a long time ago. And neither is this to say that accepting the boundaries to fly fishing means keeping the sport static. The great innovators in our sport have always contributed greatly to our fish-catching efficiency, but they've always done so by improving and broadening the realm of fly fishing, not by dumbing it down into something else. And short of trying to outline any kind of authoritative definition of fly fishing based on tackle, I do believe there is a point where we're just not fly fishing anymore, and for me, it is a conceptual distinction. Simply put, when catching fish becomes more important to us than how they are caught, we cross the line between fly fishing and just fishing; however, more to the point, in doing so, we also necessarily lose all of the rich rewards unique to our sport.

In my own case, the sense of wonder I get from fly fishing has been one of the most enduring pleasures of all my time as a fly fisher. For no matter how many fish I catch with flies, each time I do there is a small part of me that's still somewhat astounded that it even happened at all. And for me, there is a powerfully euphoric and addictive component to this feeling of astonishment, over and above the satisfaction of hooking up. Even better, I can increase the dosage of this drug by simply changing flies. For while I am indeed amazed each time I dredge up a steelhead on a big, fat, weighted, articulated leech fished deep off a heavy tip, I'm doubly blown away each time I raise one to a small October Caddis skated across the top off a dry line. The really great thing to me is that there's a world of room for this kind of tinkering with all kinds of species and types of fly fishing.

On other occasions, such as those perfect August days in a spectacular trout pool I know called Old Man's Beard, when big, wild, and utterly uneducated rainbow are gorging on the afternoon green drake hatch with total abandon, I can be completely baffled when my fly isn't taken. And while this brand of wonder doesn't come with any kind of euphoria or adrenaline hit, its effects may be equally intense, certainly more prolonged, and almost always more consuming. In fact, while we fly fishers may appear motivated by the thrill and satisfaction of hooking up, I think that ultimately we are more captivated and driven by those situations where the exact opposite happens.

On a more earthly note, the places we fly fish are often the most unspoiled and beautiful in the world. So even if the only role of fly fishing were to draw us out to these places, that in itself would be ample reason to fly fish, especially since we often find ourselves in such places with like-minded fanatics who are among the few people in our lives who need no explanation

xxvi

for our madness. But not only does fly fishing provide us the reason to go, it also give us a highly compelling means to be far more than mere spectators when we get there, regardless of our individual goals and aspirations in fly fishing. And as we all know, the power, intensity, and richness of the resulting experiences not only provide us with a complete and often necessary escape from the clutter and background noise of "real life," but also plant powerful seeds that can blossom into grand adventures to the far-flung corners of the Earth in search of more. And, it seems there are no more accepting or nurturing grounds for such seeds than in the fertile minds of fly fishers.

Thinking about all this for some unknown reason reminded me of my beloved dog, Sailor, who lived only to retrieve thrown objects. If nothing else, he was a full-blown tennis-ball addict. Indoors, he'd often take his current smelly old spit-soaked ball and roll it under some piece of furniture where he could sometimes see it but almost never reach it. And then he'd proceed to whine and scratch incessantly while trying to get at it. If I retrieved the ball for him, though, often, he'd immediately roll it back under the furniture, only to resume the whining and whimpering all over again. At first, this little act just seemed like an irritating play for attention, but more often than not, after I gave him the ball, he almost seemed to resent the interruption, even though the ball seemed to be what he wanted more than anything. But virtually every time, Sailor appeared equally content, if not happier, just to be left alone—stymied yet fully engrossed in this puzzle of his own making. If Sailor were human, I think he would have been a fly fisher.

CHAPTER 1

Southern Sea Runs

Sea Trout and Steelhead: Tierra del Fuego, Argentina

Early on in my life as a fly fisher, I encountered a prophet. Of course I didn't realize it at the time, but in fairness, who ever does? Almost by definition, that's how prophetic experiences have to go, and mine was a very subtle one at that. No parting of roiling black clouds, blinding bolts of lightning, booming claps of thunder, nor the ethereal strains of trumpeting angels accompanied the event to provide any hint whatsoever that I might, in fact, be dealing with an oracle. Young, obviously naïve, and noticeably new to the sport, I had just finished making a purchase at a local fly shop when it happened. The old guy behind the counter handed me my package, and just as I was turning to leave, fixed me with a strange and knowing look, and out of the clear blue, uttered these strange words: "You know, son, this could lead to plane tickets to Argentina."

Huh? Those words made so little sense to me back then that he might as well have been speaking in tongues. At the time, it should have been painfully obvious to anyone that plane tickets to pretty much anywhere were ridiculously beyond my budget, and Argentina was still far beyond my rather limited worldview of fly fishing. In fact, I was so completely baffled and taken aback that to this day, I don't even remember just what it was I bought that day. I do quite vividly recall feeling very awkward and uncomfortable though, sincerely wondering if the old boy hadn't indeed just blown a gasket. Hell, in those days I thought catching a bunch of little sea-run cutthroats an hour's drive from home was some pretty cool stuff.

Inevitably, though, time expanded my then narrow view of the fly-fishing world, and I, like most fly fishers, began thinking that catching a bunch of massive, sea-run browns clear on the other side of the earth might be a pretty cool gig too. And each of the countless times since then that I dreamt of fishing in Argentina, I also couldn't help but chuckle to myself at how freaked out

Estancia Maria Behety,
Tierra del Fuego, Argentina

Opposite page:
Gauchos, Estancia Maria
Behety, Tierra del Fuego,
Argentina

2

I must have looked to the old guy in the fly shop. But this day, the memory was especially strong, and I felt like laughing out loud as my plane was about to land in the small town of Rio Grande, Tierra del Fuego, Argentina, and my old sage's prophecy was being fulfilled in a fashion that I'm sure even he could have never foretold.

Below me, the wild blue waters of the southern Atlantic pounded the jagged southern Patagonian coastline. The landscape appeared surprisingly stark, brown, and austere, and the wind-whipped southern ocean looked fierce, untamed, and frigid. This really was the end of the earth, and it looked like it. But more to the point, even from the air, it gave the impression of a place where strong, wild fish should be found thriving in the rich, biological soup of the southern ocean and growing to be some of the biggest sea-run brown trout in the world. For the next two weeks, Joe, Rich, Vern, and I would embark on an amazing angling adventure here, first fishing the famous waters of the Rio Grande, then taking a four hundred-mile drive north out of Tierra del Fuego and into the rugged Patagonian countryside to sample the Rio Gallegos for more browns, and even a brief visit to the Rio Santa Cruz to investigate the Atlantic-run steelhead. So here I was, fishing the big three rivers of southern Argentina for sea-run fish and taking a long road trip that included a crossing of the infamous Straits of Magellan. The old guy at the fly shop predicted the plane tickets, but he sure didn't mention anything like this.

From the small southern town of Ciudad Rio Grande at the mouth of the river, it is just a half-hour drive upstream into the history of Patagonia itself and to our destination lodge at Estancia Maria Behety. Sprawling over 120,000 acres of the big island of Tierra del Fuego, this estancia is a mere portion of the original Estancia Primera Argentina, established in 1897. Its founder, Jose Menendez, was once known as the King of Patagonia, and his empire once encompassed some 475,000 acres of la Isla Grande, the big island of Tierra del Fuego, stretching from the Atlantic to the Chilean border. Estancia Primera Argentina covered

the north side of the Rio Grande and the Estancia Segunda Argentina, another of Jose's little holdings, the south. During their heyday, these ranches were home to 150,000 sheep. Estancia Maria Behety, named for Jose's wife, is still owned by the Menendez family. It is now a working ranch and home to the world's largest sheep-shearing shed, capable of handling five thousand head of sheep per day. Most important for anglers, though, it borders over thirty miles of some of the best fishing waters on the entire Rio Grande. Indeed, opposite Maria Behety are the other famous sea-trout lodges of Tierra del Fuego—Kau Tapen, Villa Maria, and Toon Ken—most still owned by some member of the Menendez clan.

THE RIO GRANDE

Flowing through the rolling, pampas-like steppe of northern Tierra del Fuego, the Rio Grande in this region twists through a vast treeless plain—rugged, brown, and semiarid. The landscape is breathtakingly huge, not unlike the expansive open tundra of the far north, but the skies are even bigger. And often, the limitless adventure and mystique of Patagonia seem reflected here in biblically tumultuous cloud formations sculpted by fierce southern gales and in stunningly prolonged and saturated sunrises and sunsets. On appearances alone, the river itself is somewhat at odds with all this drama and with what I had expected. I suppose

that along with the romantic notion of huge anadromous fish battling their way upstream comes a corresponding image of big brawling waters, fierce rapids, and seemingly impassable waterfalls. The Rio Grande, though, is a sleeper, almost canal-like, and when not being thrashed by the infamous gales of Patagonia, it meanders rather peacefully through the raw, sparse, wind-scoured landscape.

Over its thirty-mile course through the Estancia Maria Behety, the river is a series of runs rather than defined pools, and as such, it seems virtually all of it is fishable water. Access is by vehicle, and with this much

Sea trout, Rio Grande, Tierra del Fuego, Argentina

Opposite page:
Rio Gallegos, Argentina

5

Sea trout, Rio Grande,
Tierra del Fuego, Argentina

6

water spread over just twelve anglers, over the course of the week we never saw the same run twice. Always fishing from broad, gently sloping gravel beaches, you could wade and fish this river blindfolded, and in most places, hitting the far bank with a good double-handed cast isn't a problem. Although I'd heard that dry-fly fishing is possible here when conditions are right, we were resigned to using fairly heavy tips, and most often the guides strongly encouraged the use of surprisingly small flies. The green-bodied, rubber-legged EMB nymph was a guide favorite. Armed with standard Pacific Northwest double-handed steelhead gear and the accompanying mind-set, I found that fishing for sea trout did have surprising differences besides the use of tiny flies. Instead of a classic, dead-drift swing, the guides here favored working the fly vigorously throughout the swing, sometimes even jigging it repeatedly back and forth about a foot and a half, a move that would make most steelheaders shudder, especially when fishing a small nymph.

That said, these techniques were deadly on these southern sea-run browns, and the Rio Grande upheld its reputation as one of the great fly-fishing rivers of the world. The fish were indeed big and plentiful, averaging twelve to fifteen pounds, and on occasion, up to thirty. As the first sea trout I'd ever seen, what impressed me most was the wide variability in their appearances. Some looked just like overgrown brown trout. Others were silver-bright bars of chrome, oceanic-looking, and every fish caught seemed to be some unique variation between these two extremes. This degree of difference just isn't common in the steelhead I'm used to, and neither are fish that approach the thirty-pound mark, like the absolute hog that Rich caught late one evening. Easily the largest fish any of us caught all week, this fish took Rich on a run at least seventy-five yards downstream that lasted well into the dark of night.

The fighting habits of these fish were expected, yet impressive, and at least equal to most steelhead I've caught. They run and jump like any good sea-going salmonid should, but unlike steelhead, these southern

sea trout all seemed to take the fly decisively and with authority. And although I love how steelhead will play with a fly, not once in this week did I encounter a sea trout that tapped and tugged gingerly at the fly as steelhead sometimes do. One particularly strange example of this came from a fifteen-pound fish that I found near the tail of a run. Although we encountered no rocks of any consequence in this river, when my fly stopped

Sea trout, Rio Gallegos, Argentina

dead in mid-swing, it felt and acted for all the world like a snag. Accordingly, I threw slack line, pointed my rod straight at the fly, and yanked from different angles, but despite all my machinations, the fly never budged. While big fish can often feel like snags initially, this one stayed put for so long that in my mind, at least, it just had to be the bottom. But as I finally started walking out of the pool with the rod carelessly slung over my shoulder, intending to break the tippet, the snag suddenly pulled back. Surprised, delighted, and somewhat embarrassed, I took a quick look around for witnesses, and despite my unorthodox approach, eventually got the magnificent fish to the beach. And once it was duly clucked over, photographed, and safely released, I really thought I'd gotten away with one, but after everyone else had gone back to their rods, our guide, Diego, sauntered over and busted me. "You thought that fish was the bottom, didn't you?" he asked with a sly grin, and before I could spit out a lie, added, "I know because I was watching you from the bank."

Sometimes the rivers and fish we dream about the most are ruined in reality by the unreal expectations created in our fantasies, but luckily for me, that wasn't the case for the Rio Grande. And while the river itself wasn't as interesting as I may have imagined it to be, everything about the angling experience here really is what an exotic, world-class, destination fishing resort should reasonably provide. For one who doesn't normally equate fishing with this level of refinement in meals

and lodging, the Argentine hospitality at Maria Behety is almost uncomfortably comfortable, and the extended midday break for a large, exquisite meal, plenty of wine, and a siesta before heading out fishing again in the late afternoon is in my view such an appropriate approach to fly fishing (and perhaps life) in general that I began to wonder why we don't always do this. Patagonia is a place steeped in history and adventure and exploratory fly fishing itself, as you walk in the footsteps of legendary anglers like Joe Brooks and Jorge Donovan. And of course today, the numbers and average size of the sea trout here are unmatched anywhere else in the world.

Sea trout, Rio Grande, Tierra del Fuego, Argentina

Opposite page: Rio Gallegos, Argentina

9

Opposite page:
Rio Gallegos, Argentina

The Rio Grande in reality is what fly fishers' dreams should be made of, and with any luck, fulfilled at least once in every fly fisher's life. But in this land of angling dreams, we weren't ready to wake up just yet, so we set off on the road through Patagonia for round two.

THE RIO GALLEGOS

Over and over again, the bow of the sleek, open-decked ferry seemed to heave and fall in slow motion, each time all but disappearing under a crushing blue wave and brilliant white explosion of sea spray before rising back up out of the froth as it steadily pounded its way toward us through the infamous fury of the southern ocean. These were the storied Straits of Magellan, which separate the island of Tierra del Fuego from the South America mainland, and from the safety and security of dry land, we watched this spectacle with great interest, awe, and some anxiety, knowing we'd be on that same ferry on its return voyage in just about a half-hour's time—provided, of course, that it didn't sink before it got here. En route from Rio Grande to Rio Gallegos, we stood on the shores of Bahia Azul, Chile, silently taking stock of the situation. Powerful gales buffeted our bodies and howled in our ears, and while not a word was spoken, I suspect at this point we were all wondering why the hell we hadn't chosen to fly.

Argentina's second most famous sea-trout river is located about four hundred miles to the north of the Rio Grande on the Argentine mainland, and while slightly smaller in angling reputation, the Rio Gallegos is actually a bigger and longer river than its more famous southern counterpart. By land, it's a rough and rocky ten-hour drive over a teeth-loosening, tire-flattening, largely gravel track running through the wild, rugged, and largely uninhabited, windswept plains of southern Patagonia, into and back out of Chile, and of course, across one stretch of really nasty water. Since the island of Tierra del Fuego is shared by Chile and Argentina, and the ferry crossing to the mainland is in Chile, oddly enough, to get from one part of Argentina to another, a transit through Chile is required. We chose the open road just for the added adventure, and the ferry ride alone gave us more than we'd anticipated. The balance of the journey was well worth it too, as we saw the exotic and timeless scenes of Patagonia no one sees from the air: the occasional lone gaucho riding the open range with only his dogs as companions, herding a large flock of sheep to who knows where; strange, camel-like guanacos dotting the hillsides, and ostrich-like rheas running down the road beside us. Finally, we reached the town of Rio Gallegos, where our angling adventure was about to continue.

For the next few days, we would sample the Rio Gallegos from Estancia Guer Aike, near the mouth of the river, and Estancia Carlotta, much farther upstream, but both run by Alejandro de Tomasso and represented by the Fly Shop, and also from the Estancia Buitreras,

owned and operated by Loop Tackle. While each of these lodges and the water they fish warrants at least a week unto themselves, our time at each was short, but we were still afforded the rare opportunity to see a great deal of this somewhat unsung river.

While similar in character to the landscape of Tierra del Fuego, this part of Patagonia has much more variety and relief, with high bluffs and steep banks rising up from the valley bottom. Like the Rio Grande, the Rio Gallegos is generally gravel-bottomed, but with everything from broad, slow-flowing runs to more defined pools, fast-running narrows and riffles, this river indeed offers a much wider variety of interesting fishing water and, consequently, more opportunities for discovery. And, fishing with Christer Sjorberg of Loop, one of his top casting instructors, Mattias, and expert Argentinean guides Claudio and Pollo on the forty-kilometer stretch of the Estancia Buitreras, we were given these opportunities, shown the grace and power of the Scandinavian underhand cast, and learned a bit more of the surprising habits of the southern sea-run brown trout.

Although the strong Patagonian winds are often thought to be the biggest detriment to fishing and casting here, we learned that the lack of wind can indeed make catching these sea trout much more difficult, as it seems to make them hyper-wary and give them lockjaw. Also, while sea trout are often found in water similar to good steelhead water, I found out they also sit in water so froggy that I normally wouldn't even consider casting into it—especially double-handed. So when Pollo first put me on to such a stretch, I raised an eyebrow, said something about "agua" and "ranas" that I don't think translated very well, and gazed around the countryside halfheartedly stripping my wavy, dead fly line back in, only to miss a huge, aggressive boil on the fly that was either a sea trout or the biggest, nastiest frog that ever lived. As the old saying goes, "The jerk on the end of this line was definitely me," and I was reminded that second-guessing the guide is rarely a smart move anywhere.

Fishing with Christer on the Loop Pool one afternoon, I witnessed the most beautiful fish we saw on the Rio Gallegos in our short stay. I went through the pool first with no luck, and Christer came through not minutes behind me, hooking and landing a spectacular sixteen-pound fish that I had obviously just covered. So despite their differences, I also saw firsthand how these southern sea trout really can act a lot like steelhead sometimes.

THE RIO SANTA CRUZ

Whether they are sea trout, steelhead, or Atlantic salmon, there is a powerful mystique and allure to all sea-run salmonids that is legendary and somewhat inexplicable. But Atlantic steelhead? Indeed, our last few whirlwind days of fishing adventure in the land of the sea-run brown were spent farther north on the Rio Santa Cruz,

Opposite page:
Rio Grande, Tierra del Fuego, Argentina

13

home to the only known run of Atlantic steelhead, and as such, perhaps the most distinctive population of steelhead anywhere in the world. In fact, the steelhead fishery here has only been known at all for the past several years, when the locals in the town of Commandante Luis Piedra Buena, near the mouth of the river, began to catch the big, powerful, silvery fish at certain times of the year. So here, not only was there the powerful draw of a sea-run fish, but also the considerable allure of a young and exploratory fishery. In fact, aside from the locals and sporadic visits from foreign anglers fishing only the lower reaches of this river, the Rio Santa Cruz fishery was essentially untouched and unknown.

Born of two huge lakes fed by the massive southern ice fields of the Andes, the Rio Santa Cruz is southern Patagonia's second largest river system, running the entire breadth of the country before spilling out into the Atlantic at Puerto Santa Cruz. In its lower reaches, near Piedra Buena, it is a massive river, comparable in size to British Columbia's lower Skeena or even the Columbia. Our plan was to explore this fishery from Piedra Buena with local guides Piti Chapparo and Pablo Destefano, but just over three weeks prior to our arrival, a massive glacial ice dam on one of the river's source lakes burst, causing the mother of all blowouts. When we arrived, chunks of ice were no longer floating downstream and the water was on the drop, but the river was still abnormally high and dirty, a far cry from what might be considered ideal.

But even beyond the conditions and the great size of this river, steelheading in Patagonia was unlike any steelheading I'd ever done. The banks of the lower Santa Cruz are largely soft and muddy, sometimes with a sprinkling of gravel, and fishing here often seems like fishing the shores of a large, moving lake—hardly classic North American steelhead water, to say the least. So, while we came armed with Spey rods and few expectations, it was easy to feel both under-gunned and somewhat doubtful even to the very existence of steelhead in these waters. In fact, over three days of hard fishing, we had just three fish on, but considering the conditions and the species, that was more than enough to plant a powerful seed. Atlantic steelhead were indeed real, and the few we saw were spectacular. Since the waters here are nearly tidal, these steelhead were still sea-bright and strong. The most impressive example we saw was Vern's fish, which came at dusk of our second day of fishing—a shimmering eighteen-pound slab of silver with a characteristically pale pink blush on cheek and flanks. At this point, Vern and I wondered two main things: First, what would this fishery be in ideal water conditions, and second, what happens farther upstream on this huge and unknown steelhead stream? Indeed, the spell was cast, but that's another story altogether.

I don't exactly know what it is about sea-run fish that can so completely preoccupy our angling aspirations, often pushing them to the point of obsession. Obviously, their size and strength is a factor, as the fury they can unleash on the end of a fly line can be almost sublime in its ferocity. They are enigmatic in lifestyle and behavior—at once voracious ocean predator and secretive, bug-sipping trout, highly aggressive, yet sometimes almost impossible to catch. And whatever the case, perhaps their most insidious characteristic is that each one we encounter seems not to satisfy nor quell the obsession at all, but only to intensify it. Southern sea-runs are no exception. In fact, they may even represent a more potent form of the drug. For combined with all the considerable allure of the sea-run fish is the exotic history, culture, and adventure of Argentina and Patagonia—the land of Tango, gauchos, polo, beef, red wine, sprawling estancias, and the unlimited promise of wind-whipped adventures at the southernmost tip of the Americas. So whether you've visited Argentina or not, always keep in mind that the next purchase you make at your local fly shop, whatever it might be, could very well lead to plane tickets to this country. And with any luck, it will, over and over again. *Buena suerte, y buen viaje.*

CHAPTER 2

Nirvana on the Nass
Steelhead: British Columbia

There is a distinct Zen dimension to steelheading. It is contemplative, meditative angling. After all, these mysterious, sea-run uber-rainbows have been referred to by some as "the fish of a thousand casts," and if this pessimistic forecast is even close to the truth, then what better use could there be for all that free time but to chew on a profound thought or two between fish? Indeed, if you hang around steelheaders enough, you could even get the impression sometimes that achieving true steelhead satori might actually be more about reading water, communing with your cast, getting in rhythm with the river rocks, and becoming one with the swing of your fly than it is about actually catching the fish. The steelhead, like the sound of one hand clapping, assumes the role of just another confounding koan to be solved on the path to a peculiar, piscatorial enlightenment of sorts. Furthermore, if the steelheaders in your company are members of the Spey-casting sect, this impression may very well be ampli-

fied, especially when it comes to the casting part. In this light, one might even be convinced to see each steelhead stream as a kind of lamasery, a sacred place of learning and reverence where devotees of this peculiar angling community are drawn to seek synchrony with the steelhead experience, thereby achieving divine separation from the weight of worldly clutter troubling their mortal souls.

THE NASS

This fall day, we were four such disciples seeking steelhead truth in just such a place—but one far different than most. We were enveloped in the bosom of a steelhead Shangri-la—serene, remote, pristine, and virtually unknown to the outside world. We had found an undiscovered paradise nestled deep within an enchanted wilderness and protected among a fortress of towering, snow-covered peaks—exactly the sort of setting in which you might expect to find a secret lamasery, as well as a few quirky folks. Unlike some hidden Tibetan temple, our shrine was cloaked in the quintessential Pacific Northwest palate of mossy greens, steely blues, and damp, dripping grays, all draped in a mysterious shroud of low-lying mist and fog. Despite the inherent serenity of our setting and circumstance, however, at this moment on this day there was no harmony in our humor. Peace and pensive perseverance had been rudely muscled out by chaos and consternation, creating discord and imbalance in our lives. Our horizons, however momentarily, were truly lost. We were troubled in paradise.

Geoff Straight, our guide and host from Bell II Lodge, was standing silent, barely knee-deep in the current with his arms hanging limply at his sides, river water still dripping from his face and hands. Vern stood just a few feet away, almost imperceptibly slumped over and equally meditative, his fourteen-foot Spey rod and overall spirit suddenly drained of the considerable life force and tension that had coursed through them both just a split second ago. In our minds' eyes we could all still see the agent of that force—a big steelhead, right at our feet, hovering motionless over the smooth river rocks in just about a foot of water, suspended in what was certainly a defining moment of his own. He was at that moment free, but his primitive, pea-sized brain hadn't quite realized it yet. Despite the relative difference in brain size, though, the fish reached enlightenment before any of us, and with a mere twitch of his

tail, vanished. We were left standing there, pondering an illusion.

Vern had just lost (busted off, if the truth be known) a huge and handsome male steelie over twenty pounds that for some could have been the fish of a lifetime. To make matters worse, this was no long-line release, nor was it a textbook fish-landing attempt either. Whatever the case, we all got a good long gawk at this fish, and Geoff even grabbed it a couple of times. It wasn't just big; up until mere moments ago it was real. So real, in fact, that as the fight was all but won, we could almost feel the heft of its powerful silvery bulk as it was lifted from the water. Joe and I had even taken it one step further than that—we could already see a photograph of it in Vern's hands, gracing the cover of some future issue of *Wild On The Fly*. The only reality we were left with, however, was debilitating disappointment, and we were struck speechless by a multitude of emotions: couldas and shouldas, and instant replays from every conceivable angle, which simultaneously played in our heads, causing gridlock in our gray matter.

After what seemed like an eternal silence, Joe was the first to regain the ability to speak. Very quietly, and in a carefully measured tone, he asked, "Is that the prescribed method for landing a big steelhead?" Since the fish was obviously lost, this was a trick question—another one of those nonsensical, truth-seeking riddles. By then, though, we were no longer in the mood to be philosophical, and Joe's crafty question triggered a rather violent response, transforming us from a muted,

Opposite page:
Upper Nass River, British
Columbia, Canada

somewhat mature group of anglers to a loud and angry little mob. In fact, we pretty much came completely unglued, launching into an outburst of expletives, explanations, admonitions, and unsolicited advice that bore little resemblance to a sincere search for the truth but rather, sounded a lot like bickering. Our steelhead had become the fish of a thousand curses.

Completing our utter diversion from the liquid path of enlightenment to the rocky road to hell, this chaotic outburst swiftly resolved itself into one very pointed directive. Ironically, it was aimed squarely at poor Vern— the guy who hooked the fish in the first place, and therefore, was the only one of us who had really suffered any kind of a loss whatsoever. Our unreasonable little tirade ignored this fact and carried an almost punitive connotation. "Just get the hell back in there and get us another one!" is what it amounted to. It was almost as if Vern had cheated *us* of something, and we were demanding retribution. Nothing unreasonable of course, we just wanted *another* twenty-pound steelhead. The other somewhat interesting fact that was recklessly ignored is that in a previous lifetime Vern played in the Rose Bowl as a linebacker for the Washington Huskies. People in more complete control of their faculties would most certainly have chosen a far more diplomatic approach to Vern—especially at a time like that.

Luckily for us, however, Vern simply tied on another fly, silently stepped back into the water, and lo and behold, another twenty-pound steelhead is exactly what he produced. Indeed, just two casts and not even

twenty feet further down the run, he hooked up on another big steelie, and this time it was landed. Brother Vern's karma was obviously intact, and for the second time this day, we were rendered speechless. This time, though, serenity seeped back into our souls, balance was restored to our secret little valley, and just like that we were whole once more, going from paradise to purgatory and back again quicker than you could say *Onchorynchus mykiss* twice in rapid succession.

Now, whether you want to call it karma, mojo, masterful skill, blind luck, or a combination thereof, something was certainly at work here, since back-to-back twenty-pound steelhead is truly an unbelievable, some might say miraculous occurrence. After all, just one twenty-pounder is a pretty big deal in itself, as it represents a rite of passage among the steelhead faithful. More precisely, once you've caught one, you can, in good conscience, go to the grave thinking of yourself as a true steelheader. Up until then, you're just sort of apprenticing—or so I'm often told. As for numbers, while the high priests of this calling do seem to repeat multiple fish days with magical consistency, even for them, back-to-back twenties are virtually unheard of. As for the rest of us, two steelhead of any size hooked in an entire day, let alone brought to the beach within a couple of casts, would realistically be considered a pretty fair outing. Fortunately, though, for those of us still sitting low in this complicated hierarchy, there is one obvious way to accelerate our ascent through the ranks, which thankfully has little to do with personal

virtue or angling virtuosity. That is, fishing in waters holding large numbers of big steelhead with virtually no other anglers trying to mess with them really helps a lot. And this is exactly what our utopia was all about.

Vern's back-to-back twenties came on a run named Double Digit that lies at the remote confluence of the upper Nass and Damdochax rivers in northwestern British Columbia. As its name suggests, it is arguably as fine a stretch of steelhead water that this province has to offer, which admittedly is a pretty grandiose statement. However, its location and subsequent quality of fishing makes it a pretty unique piece of steelhead real estate and the figurative, if not geographical, heart of

Upper Nass River, British Columbia, Canada

Opposite page:
Upper Nass River, British Columbia, Canada

21

22

this little known region of steelhead plenty.

"The first time we fished this run was just last year [2002] in our first heli-fishing package ever," Geoff explained. "My two clients, Cliff Watts and Joe Macy, wanted to check it out, so we flew in here. I hooked up within my first few casts, so I mentioned to one of the guys that it could be a double-digit day if this was any indication of how good this place really was. It was incredible. In the next three hours, we hooked sixteen and landed eleven, hence the name: Double Digit."

For the very few fanatical and erudite steelheaders in the world who have even heard of the Nass or Damdochax rivers, these results may come as no big surprise. For those who haven't, this fish story should be a lot easier to swallow knowing that the Nass, in a salmonid sense, is essentially the reclusive little brother of the world renowned Skeena. After all, trying to imagine a steelheader who is ignorant of the Skeena and its spectacular tributaries is a bit like trying to conjure up a Catholic who's never heard of the Vatican. From this perspective, the relative anonymity of the neighboring Nass is quite curious, since both these rivers are born in the same high, heavily glaciated peaks of the Skeena Mountains and run a roughly parallel course to the Pacific. In fact, the Nass is British Columbia's third largest river coming right after—you guessed it—the Skeena.

The superficial explanation for this state of affairs is that much of the water of the Skeena system has an important highway running closely parallel to it, as well as scores of secondary roads, giving lodge operators and guides ample access to the river. In direct contrast, the Nass, except in its lower reaches, is still protected by a virtually impenetrable wilderness, which allows the upper Nass and its two most important tributaries, the Damdochax and Bell Irving rivers, to remain essentially unknown. Furthermore, at some time in the Bell Irving's murky history, an observant correspondent tagged it as "unfishable" because of excessive glacial influence. Over time, this assessment evolved into conventional wisdom and has even made it into print. For interest's sake, I dug up an old British Columbia fishing atlas not quite ten years old that confirmed it all in black and white. The entry for the Skeena begins, "This river and its many tributaries provide the greatest river fishing undoubtedly in the province." Despite the peculiar wording, most would likely agree with this assessment. The entries for the Nass and Bell Irving, however, are decidedly less encouraging, both ending with the same two words: "Seldom fishable." The Damdochax isn't even listed.

Our portal into this mysterious world of unfishable and unknown waters was Bell II Lodge, which sits just over two hundred miles by road north of the town of Terrace, British Columbia, and is named for the place where the Cassiar Highway crosses the Bell Irving River for the second time. Sandwiched between the Coast Mountains to the west and the Skeena Range to the east, this region is about as backwoods British Columbia as you can get on a paved road. Out here, you're more likely to be involved in an accident with

a moose or a bear than another vehicle, so the mere existence of a facility like Bell II is initially something of a mystery in itself.

The first face of Bell II you encounter is an incongruous combination of a typical "last chance for gas till Alaska" filling station, which has what looks like a funky, oversized, almost Bavarian-style coffee shop attached to it. Upon closer examination, you realize that there is also nothing less than an entire, well-manicured little Euro-style village behind the coffee shop, comprising several large and luxurious log chalets. These chalets, in turn, surround a stone building capped with a curious sod roof that houses an exercise room, gym, and sauna.

Steelhead, Nass River, British Columbia, Canada

Opposite page: Bell-Irving River, British Columbia, Canada

23

Steelhead, Damdochax River,
British Columbia, Canada

pany, Last Frontier HeliSkiing, bought this property in 1999, and since then has invested over $5 million and created one of the world's top destination heli-skiing resorts. Operating on the largest recreational land tenure in British Columbia, the site already boasts over 450 named runs, ranging from steep tree-and-glade runs to high alpine glacier skiing, most of which sits just minutes by helicopter from the lodge amid the impressive peaks of the surrounding Skeena Range. After an exploratory fishing season in 1999, Geoff spearheaded this operation's off-season expansion to include access to a world-class steelhead fishery the following year. Their established helicopter base made access to the remote upper Nass and Damdochax rivers a reality, and by adding jet boats to the mix, Bell II Lodge made the "unfishable" waters of the Bell Irving River home.

As Geoff puts it, "The Bell's really our bread and butter. We can fish up to sixty kilometers of it by jet boat, and access the upper twenty kilometers by helicopter, but so far, we've just focused on the twenty kilometers or so around the launch. In just this stretch, alone, we've already named over forty runs, and there are still a lot more pools that are un-named."

He is also quick to credit the help and experience of Wally Faetz and Ken Moreau, the owners of Spey Lodge in Terrace, for help with learning and opening up this frontier fishery. Wally and Ken are the only other operators who consistently take fly-fishing clients on this river, and when they do, they use Bell II Lodge as their base of operations.

Directly adjacent is a large deck and log gazebo covering a party-sized hot tub. It is an oasis of opulence in the middle of nowhere with no immediately apparent raison d'etre. The filling station you can understand, but you can't help but wonder just what all the other fancy stuff is here for. The explanation is that Bell II, aside from actually being a roadside fuel stop, is first and foremost a heli-skiing lodge. In fishing season, though, before the snow flies, this can all look terribly out of place.

First impressions aside, heli-skiers do know how to live, and successful heli-ski operators like the folks at Bell II know how to accommodate them. The parent com-

In the few seasons they've been exploring this river, it has become apparent that in prime condition the Bell Irving produces numbers and sizes of fish that compare very favorably with many of its famous Skeena neighbors. Also, as in many of those waters, the fish here will rise freely to skated drys, which for some represents the pinnacle of the steelhead experience (whether the fish actually eats the fly or not). Unlike most of the Skeena waters, however, the Bell Irving is still the kind of river where if you hit a good run on a good day, you have a legitimate shot at steelhead immortality, as more than likely they'll be able to name the run in your honor.

Our week on the Bell Irving was the first of the season and, unfortunately, the river wasn't in prime condition. Increased glacial runoff caused by unseasonably warm temperatures combined with intermittent rain had compromised the water clarity. The river was definitely fishable, but dry flies were pretty much out of the question. Adding to the challenge, three among our party of seven anglers were first-time steelheaders and also new to double-handed rods. So, while no new runs were named this week, the Bell Irving still produced fairly consistently, giving up between three and ten steelhead each day to just four rods.

Just as the Bell Irving is this operation's bread and butter, the helicopter program into the upper Nass and Damdochax is the gravy. These waters are truly accessible only by helicopter, and the flight alone from Bell II through the Skeena mountains is spectacular enough to make you forget about fishing altogether. If looking up at the jagged, snow-covered peaks towering above the puny helicopter you're in doesn't take your breath away, then looking down at the broad, powerful wings of eagles soaring below you and perhaps even at a big fat grizzly lumbering through a virgin stand of old-growth pine forest most certainly will. Directly upstream from the Bell Irving confluence, the Nass careers its way through a wide, heavily forested valley in a long stretch of narrow canyon. In fact from the air this canyon looks so long and gnarly that it's difficult to believe any salmon or steelhead attempting the passage wouldn't eventually be spit out the other end of the nasty chute as battered pulp—the prime reason Geoff contends that only the biggest, strongest steelies make it up here. Upstream of the canyon, however, the upper Nass twists through gentler terrain in a seemingly endless series of pools, runs, and sweeping gravel bars that serve to snap you back from awestruck sightseer to anxious steelheader in a mere fraction of a second.

So far, Bell II has focused on just a tiny stretch of the upper river, beginning just above Double Digit and the Nass-Damdochax confluence and extending just about three miles downstream. Guests generally fly into the Hen Run at the top and are rowed down the Nass in a raft through what Geoff estimates are over twenty distinct runs, most of which are just waiting to be named. In the course of our week, weather permitting, three anglers per day made the flight into the upper Nass. You already know what happened there with Vern and

Joe. On a separate occasion, I flew in with Joe Macy, a highly experienced angler and Colorado trout guide, and Loc Vetter, one of the first-time steelheader/Spey casters I mentioned previously. At our first stop at the Hen Run, Joe started off by catching a couple of nice Dolly Vardens at the head of the run, and near the tail, Loc landed his first ever steelhead.

We then hopped over to Double Digit, where Geoff and pilot Sid Peltier dropped us off and then left to reposition the raft and some other gear with the helicopter. Having witnessed Vern's performance here just the day before, I was primed for a big day and couldn't wait to get into the water. Loc obviously had other ideas. He started to really click with the Spey rod, and while I was trying to fish down behind him, I ended up spending most of my time helping him land and release three more nice steelies in front of me and watching him hook and lose at least two more. Of course all the beauties Loc landed also needed to be photographed, so he did a pretty fair one-man job of keeping me off the water altogether. If this wasn't enough, sometime during Loc's flurry of fishing activity, I noticed Joe Macy about a hundred yards upstream at the very head of the run with a deeply bent rod, so I hoofed it up there just in time to help him land a fresh female in the eighteen- to twenty-pound range that was probably the most spectacular fish I saw all week. This is how the morning started on a day when the Nass ended up yielding thirteen steelhead to our group of three anglers. Over dinner that night back at Bell II, we also

learned that the Bell Irving had yielded ten more fish to the four anglers who fished there this day. Not a bad showing for a couple of "seldom fishable" rivers.

Joking aside, both the Nass and the Bell Irving, like many of the steelhead streams in this part of the country, are indeed glacially fed and influenced. Warmer temperatures do mean increased turbidity, and on occasion, these rivers can indeed become unfishable. The fact of the matter is, whether by rain or glacial runoff, steelhead streams the world over get blown out from time to time. Indeed, perfect water conditions are probably the exception rather than the rule, which may be another reason steelheaders are a rather philosophical bunch. So, although Bell II has only been fishing these "unfishable" waters for a few seasons, the total days lost because of water conditions are no more or less than any similar stream in this part of the country. In addition, Bell II's helicopter capability is the ultimate ace in the hole, as it makes access to the neighboring Craig, Iskut, or even the Stikine possible—all rivers which host healthy runs of salmon and steelhead. And indeed, if there's ever a day in this neck of the woods where you can't find a fishable salmon stream with a helicopter, that's probably the day you should start building an ark.

THE DAMDOCHAX

The Damdochax rounded out the trilogy of the somewhat misunderstood rivers of our secret Shangri-la, and if Double Digit could be considered the heart of

Opposite page:
Steelhead, Upper Nass River, British Columbia, Canada

27

this region, then the Damdochax is its very soul. Fed by Damdochax Lake just twelve miles upstream of its confluence with the Nass, this river, unlike both the Bell Irving and the Nass, is not influenced by glacial runoff, and with the stabilizing effects of the lake, generally runs clear. Also, in contrast to the bigger Nass and Bell Irving waters, which beg for big, booming Spey casts, the Damdochax is a small and intimate forest stream where in most places there seems hardly enough room to swing a cat, let alone a long double-handed rod. In fact, the forest here is often so close and thick to the water that even walking streamside with a fourteen-foot rod can be a challenge in itself. In contrast to its size, however, the diminutive Damdochax is probably the single most important tributary in the entire upper Nass system, supporting very healthy runs of chinook, coho, and sockeye salmon, as well as resident populations of good-size rainbows and Dolly Varden, and bull trout. Also a good percentage of the big steelhead in the entire upper Nass, like those we found stacked up at Double Digit, are indeed homing in on this little stream. In salmon season, as you might expect, this aquatic bounty also attracts a fairly robust run of very good-size grizzly bears—some of whom are even known by name.

To whom they are known is yet another one of the mysterious twists to this region, for as if to mirror its seemingly disproportionate biological significance, the Damdochax also boasts a fairly unique human presence, namely, Alice and Hannah Belford, the mother and daughter team who own and operate Damdochax River Lodge along with a small but dedicated staff. People are about the last things you'd expect to find here, let alone a mother and daughter fishing team, but the Belfords have been introducing people to this "high energy area," as they call it, for over twenty-five years, which, among other things, has to make Damdochax River Lodge one of the best kept fishing secrets in all of British Columbia. Somehow, this small, long-standing operation has developed the curious combination of a devoted clientele (some of whom have fished here religiously for over a decade) as well as a cloak of secrecy that would make the Pentagon proud.

Far from the world of jet boats, helicopter pads, and hot tubs, here you live by the warmth of woodstoves and the mellow amber light of kerosene lamps in a pure, back-to-basics, low-impact program that couldn't be more perfectly suited to this pristine wilderness location. It's the kind of place and program that puts the unlikely pairing of Thoreau and steelhead in the same train of thought, as Damdochax River Lodge is the steelheading equivalent of Walden Pond, if you can imagine such a thing. The main camp of the lodge is notched into the old-growth forest overlooking the peaceful waters of small Damdochax Lake. It consists of a small, timber-framed lodge, a historic log cabin that is a remnant of the Collins Overland Telegraph, a workshop, and a few other tents and small buildings. Anglers generally split their time between this lodge and a slightly smaller river camp of tent frames perched above one of the best pools on this river situated about a two-hour hike downstream—and that's exactly how they get there. Both camps are rustic wilderness retreats in the finest and most authentic sense and are kept in such impeccable trim that there is an almost museum-like quality to them. Your personal comfort is never in question. Indeed, the luxuries here are those of simplicity and solitude, which truly enable you to derive the maximum pleasure from the wilderness setting. Damdochax River Lodge is fly fishing unplugged, the kind of place that puts us back in touch with the most essential and seductive attributes of our sport, and those that most likely drew us to it in the first place. Now in case you're wondering if I ingested some kind of hallucinogenic forest mushroom while I was here, I'll just say that if a visit doesn't make you a bit (or a lot) spiritual about fly-fishing for steelhead and connecting to all that is wild and natural in this world, you are beyond hope and should perhaps consider readjusting your schedule to include more artificial pursuits, like golf. Otherwise, you almost owe yourself a visit to a place like this if only to have your values compass recalibrated.

On this small, fecund river, the pools are well defined and seemingly made for one person at a time. And here, rather than standing in water above your belly button and stressing your rotator cuffs by trying to crack out ninety-plus feet of double-handed Spey cast (the previous term double Spey refers to a particular cast), sometimes the guide tells you to stop six feet from the water and crouch down spring-creek style, and then says something like, "Cast to the top end of that log sticking out on the opposite bank. There's usually one sitting right there" . . . all of forty feet away. This is not your standard approach to steelhead, to say the least, and it can actually be a bit confounding at first. A further ten-minute chat with head guide Hannah, however, reveals just how different the Damdochax situation can be. "A lot of the time, we sight-cast to our steelhead," she told me matter-of-factly. "I walk along the bank, spot the fish, and tell my angler where to cast. Sometimes I have to tell him when to strike, 'cause I can see that the fish has taken the fly and I can see the angler doesn't know that's even happened." Tell me that's not just a little bit different.

Since our time on the Damdochax was limited, we unfortunately didn't get to see any steelhead in the water or otherwise, so I don't have a fish story to tell you. For that, I had to pull a few snippets from Alice's weekly Web reports of what happened on various days in the 2003 season. Like Hannah's accounts, they are fairly matter-of-fact. After years of being here, this stuff is obviously normal to them. Here's a small random sampling: "Ted casts six times and catches five steelhead at the Slomo . . . Ron hooked eight steelhead and landed four of them today . . . Bruce hooks four steelhead and lands three . . . Deanna has a steelhead try to take a dry fly at the Slomo. Another examined her fly four times before it left. . . ." While this concentration of steelhead may be the prime reason to visit Damdochax River Lodge, there are many more attractions. The season here actually starts with a chinook fishery in early August and moves on to a week

29

Opposite page:
Upper Nass River, British
Columbia, Canada

or two of bear-viewing in mid to late August, before entering the prime steelhead months of September and October. Trout fishing here at times is world-class as well. And finally, despite the variety and outstanding quality of the fishing, the main emphasis here is unquestionably on the bigger picture, on the rich intangibles that have really nothing to do with fish but for which angling is just the vehicle. (I swear, no mushrooms.)

The most significant point about this entire region and all its streams is not so much the numbers and size of the fish, but how few people are fishing for them. So, despite the impression I may have given you so far, I'm really not at all hung up on naming runs. It's just that while named runs do represent a rich part of the tradition of our sport, they also represent past discoveries. The point is that today, being able to drift through perfect pools on rivers the quality of the Bell Irving and upper Nass that are essentially undiscovered (i.e., un-named) is really the true and exceedingly rare luxury this region affords.

Vern, Joe, and I had one last more opportunity to fish Double Digit together near the end of our trip. By then we'd spent almost a week in our secret Shangri-la working on our casting and karma, which also included a short, soul-straightening stay at the high altar of the Damdochax. If we had gotten any more serene or in synch with our wilderness surroundings, we might well have turned into river rocks ourselves. Therefore, rather than bickering at each other this time, our more enlightened state enabled us to engage in an eloquent

dialogue that resulted in a sanguine prediction rather than a shrill, crabby exchange.

For most of this day, the skies had been low, dark gray, and ominous. We had agreed, however, that as Vern approached the end of the run, the clouds would part, sunlight would stream through and spotlight the golden fall cottonwoods on the far shore, and he would meld with another large and handsome steelhead. All these elements, we divined, would then allow themselves to come together in a spectacular photograph for the cover of *Wild On The Fly*. And admittedly, while we were leaning heavily on Vern's status as one of the high priests of the steelhead order, this is exactly what happened. For ye of little faith, I hereby swear on my favorite Spey rod and with three wise guys (Geoff, Vern, and Joe) as my witnesses, that that is the total steelhead truth.

So, I suppose if there's any kind of enlightened wisdom to be passed on here, this is it: the next time you are out steelheading, remember to release the negative energy, stress, and general background noise created by an overemphasis on the importance of catching a fish and embrace the total suchness of the steelhead. It's all about karma anyway. Commune with your cast, become one with the swing of your fly, think only pure and profound thoughts, and the forces of the cosmos will take care of the rest. Of course, all of this cosmic crap will work a whole lot better if you try it somewhere on the Bell Irving, Damdochax, or Upper Nass rivers. May the force be with you.

CHAPTER 3

Rumble in the Jungle
Peacock Bass: Amazonas, Brazil

If peacock bass had hair, it would most likely be shaved into radical, spiked-out Mohawks and dyed bright purple to go along with their crazy, blood-red eyes and vividly neon-green bodies. They are to fish as Sid Vicious was to musicians: piscine punks—aquatic anarchists with an outrageous outward appearance and attitude to match. With each one that comes to hand, you're almost surprised to find it has no facial piercings other than your fly. Get the picture? They are the undisputed bad boys of the Brazilian jungle, and everything about them is just plain shocking.

We are slowly paddling along one of the remote backwater tributaries of the Rio Negro in north central Brazil. If this isn't the deepest, darkest heart of the world's largest tropical jungle, it's at least the sternum, and my GPS has us positioned just over one degree south of the equator. The midday sun is directly overhead, and I feel like I'm serving a sentence in some kind of karmic

payback for one of those ants I toasted under a magnifying glass as a kid. The air is still and the heat has put all the jungle sounds to rest. At high noon, even the shadows run for cover, so there is absolutely no respite from the pounding, punishing temperature. Although we are supposedly entering the rainy season in the mother of all tropical rainforests, the relative humidity is surprisingly low. You know, it's a dry heat. An eerie, baking stillness surrounds us as we glide over the tepid, coffee-colored waters snaking through the dense surrounding jungle, and I'm working the shoreline, blind-casting a ten-weight rod. The hiss of the line through the guides and the periodic paddle strokes from astern are all that break the searing outward silence, while Carlos Santana supernaturally grooves on in my head: "And it's a hot one, like seven inches from the midday sun."

Ka-boom! Suddenly, as if at the flick of a switch, a huge and startling explosion erupts along the shore-

Rio Negro, Amazonas, Brazil

Opposite page:
Rio Negro, Amazonas, Brazil

line. Water and small fish of every description are flying everywhere, as if someone bombed the tropical fish section of your local pet shop. Some of the fleeing fish fly by at eye level, easily sailing fifteen feet before arcing back into safer water. A rooster tail two feet high bursts along the bank in ten inches of water as the peacock or peacocks responsible for this outburst show their backs as they unleash the ambush. A similar effect might be achieved by throwing your kid's fish tank off the roof. We've all seen fish chasing other fish before, but this is something else. The peacocks have instantaneously turned oppressive calm into panicked, violent mayhem and created the kind of melee that, were people involved, would include a lot of yelling and screaming.

Airuma, our guide, however, was the only one screaming—and in Portuguese to boot. "Tucunaré! Grangé! Grangé!" he yelled, urging me to cast by waving his hand toward the pandemonium. As if I could have missed it. In all fairness, though, it may very well have appeared like that to him, since there is every likelihood I was standing wide-eyed, slack-jawed, and stiff, absolutely dumbfounded by the spectacle. The peacocks had changed our world in an instant. A moment ago, I'd felt like I was standing in a dry sauna, waving a two-by-four around. Now, that two-by-four had seemingly transformed itself into a limp, slow toothpick, hardly fast or strong enough for the task at hand, which was to lob a huge, water-soaked,

red-and-white streamer the size and weight of a small dishrag directly into the epicenter of the madness.

Splat! Somehow, the fly landed close to the ruckuss just as it was waning, and I started stripping like there was no tomorrow. Strip. Strip. Strip. Stop. The water boiled ten feet beyond the end of the fly line, and presto, I was hooked up to an absolutely pissed and airborne peacock bass cartwheeling across the surface in all its bright green glory.

There's an abundance of adrenaline and a decided absence of subtlety in hooking giant peacocks on the fly. On more than one occasion, I watched poppers get slammed two feet off the surface by peacocks in missed attempts. The modus operandi of these fish is better described as "smash-and-grab" or "hit-and-run" than "take," in the sense that if you're not careful, they'll take everything—fly, line, rod, and all.

Their first flight to deep water or structure is usually a blistering dash—heavy and fast but seldom into the backing. Often they go furiously airborne right off the grab, and trying to stop them at this stage is a recipe for line-burned fingers and a popped tippet or both. The rest of the fight is usually a series of heavy, sustained bursts that carry incredible weight, considering the actual size of the fish. An absolutely huge peacock bass is only twenty pounds or so, but when it decides to pull, it can, in spurts, feel closer to fifty. And in between the bursts, they rocket skyward defiantly right up until

you've got a death-grip on the lower jaws of their cavernous yaps. Even then, considering the sheer violence of the enraged tantrum they've just thrown on the end of your line, the glare that emanates from their bright, beady, crimson eyes is fairly unsettling. It really is a jungle out there.

Rio Negro, Amazonas, Brazil

Opposite page:
Rio Negro, Amazonas, Brazil

MANAUS

Snaking through this jungle are the black waters of the Rio Negro, one of the two main tributaries the mighty Amazon River, which begins just beyond the city of Manaus, Brazil, at the confluence of the Rio Negro and Rio Solimoes. Still about a thousand miles from the sea, these two huge rivers join here to form the world's largest volume of flowing freshwater, which is thought to account for one-fifth of all the continental runoff on earth. At its mouth, the Amazon is over two hundred miles wide. The Rio Negro alone, in terms of discharge, is the world's second largest river, and at its mouth near Manaus, it is some nine miles across. Even this far inland, this slow-moving freshwater flow is more like an ocean than a river, and even by the conservative estimate of more than 2,500 known and identified species of fish found here, the river system supports a greater diversity of fishes than the Atlantic. The presence of freshwater dolphins makes everything seem all the more incredible, especially since one of the two species is pink, hence the nickname "bubble gum dolphin."

Our adventure began here in Manaus, the remote northern capital of the Brazilian province of Amazonas. Fueled by the rubber boom in the late 1800s, this city flourished as an isolated yet glittering outpost of wealth and civilization, thanks to a monopoly on latex tapped from the native rubber trees. As legend has it, in its heyday some of the wealthy citizens of the city even sent their laundry away to be done in Europe. A hint

of this bygone era of decadence remains here today in the form of the *Teatro Amazonas*, or the Manaus Opera House, the city's most enduring landmark. Ostentatious, luxurious, and breathtakingly European, this hall was built entirely from materials imported from Europe, save the wood on the floors and chairs. The exclamation point on this excessive enterprise has to be that even the local wood was sent to Europe to be worked before it was installed, traveling down and back through a nearly impenetrable jungle, along a river infested with crocodiles and patrolled by jaguars. Such were the excesses

Peacock Bass, Rio Negro, Amazonas, Brazil

Opposite page:
Peacock Bass, Rio Negro, Amazonas, Brazil

40

made possible by tree sap for the wealthy few in a city of just thirty thousand inhabitants. Today, this city of 1.5 million people is a shadow of its former glory, and the only monopoly they seem to have now is on incredibly cheesy drawings of peacock bass. *Tucunaré* are important as table fare, and a tacky rendition of one adorns the sign of each and every café or restaurant that includes it on the menu. The popularity of peacocks on the plate is indeed one of the reasons that we must steam two-and-a-half days upstream by riverboat from here to get to really good peacock water.

It was 4:30 a.m. and the Varig Airlines direct flight from Miami had just disgorged its cargo of bleary-eyed travelers. This flight should have been called the Bassmaster Express, as the entire 747 was jammed with anglers, most of whom were loaded to the teeth with spinning gear and a good old Southern drawl. That fact alone wasn't surprising, since fly-fishing for peacock bass is not common practice. So, while most sport fishing operations here do cater largely to conventional-gear anglers, Amazon Fly Fishing Expeditions (AFFE) obviously takes a different tack. The founders, Octavio Campos Salles, Peter Gorinski, and Manuel (Mané) Figuera, came together with many years of experience and passion for exploring adventure angling in the most remote regions of both Brazil and Guyana, and their program in the far-flung reaches of the Rio Negro is one of the fruits of their passion. AFFE's unique program promised an ideal situation for big peacocks on

Peacock Bass, Rio Negro,
Amazonas, Brazil

Opposite page:
Peacock Bass, Rio Negro,
Amazonas, Brazil

41

the fly and was summed up in an interesting fashion in a pre-trip e-mail from Octavio. Besides requesting some details on the fishing, I had asked his opinion on the prudence of bringing my absolute, top-of-the-list fishing partner along, since she happens to be a woman. Here is the most salient part of his reply:

"You just want to make sure that she knows that this is an expedition style of trip. For instance we sleep on hammocks or small camping beds, there is no air-conditioning (the nights are usually pretty cool anyway). But this doesn't mean that the trip is rough. Most anglers going agree that it is not rough and not dangerous at all,

and the rewards are usually well worth anything. We get to fish in waters that no one ever fishes. If she is an experienced angler, I am sure she won't have any trouble with the accommodations and the style of the trip."

I should note here that I was never worried about Lisa. She is a highly experienced angler, runs a wilderness fishing lodge in British Columbia, travels better than a dirty little secret, and above all, whines infinitely less and smells infinitely better than any male fishing buddy alive. She can handle anything, but I was glad to know all the same that she would be welcome. Octavio's assessment of the relative safety and comforts of this expedition was the interesting part, especially his phrase "and the rewards are *usually* well worth anything." I was of course keen to fish the unfished Amazon, eager for the adventure into this exotic wilderness, and figured I was up to finding out what the "anything" in "well worth anything" entailed.

Lisa had reached Manaus before me, and as Octavio introduced himself at the arrival gate, he assured me she was safely asleep at the hotel and passed me a note she'd sent that read: "Had wine accident. Buy more, get smokes and any other hard liquor you think we might need." The note was indeed a bit of a surprise, but not as big a one as Octavio himself. Whereas I was half expecting a gnarly looking Amazon jungle dude with a machete on his hip, Octavio turned out instead to be a skinny, clean-cut, twenty-one-year-old kid clutching a leather valise and looking a whole lot more like a college student in a commerce program than a seasoned jungle bushwhacker. This fact notwithstanding, in the first of countless vital tasks that he would perform for us over the next two weeks, even at this ungodly hour he steered me and Big Tom (a fellow angler from New Jersey) to an open wine and liquor shop where we stocked up on two weeks worth of smokes and booze, and whisked through a still sleeping Manaus to the Hotel Brasil, all in about forty-five minutes.

I dragged Lisa out of bed, and as we smoked Brazilian cigarettes out on the tiny balcony of our eight-floor hotel room, learned how our wine had got smashed en route from Sao Paolo, and in the pale morning light, we got our first look at the impressive tiled dome of the opera house a mere two blocks away. Then when Lisa sleepily asked, "Did you see the River on your way in," we both realized the ironic fact that the key feature of the region still eluded us. Somehow, we'd both managed to arrive at different times to the banks of this almost incomprehensibly massive river, yet neither of us had so far spied so much as a single drop of flowing water. That, however, was the standard calm-before-the-storm sort of irony, as for the next two weeks, we were entirely engulfed by the watery world of Amazonas.

Later that afternoon, Octavio had us and our gear stuffed into a couple of cabs and zooming through the bewildering traffic of Manaus en route to the river port to meet our ride and home for the next fortnight. The port was a chaotic and exotic carnival of brightly painted, shallow-draft, African Queen-like river boats, most of them double-deckers about sixty feet long, clustered around a single floating wharf stretching out perpendicular to the beach. Dark-skinned kids splashed gleefully in the shallows, colorful tarps fluttered off all the boats, and a stream of people and all manner of cargo bustled back and forth from the float to the eclectic collection of vehicles parked on the beach and the riverside street. Before we knew it, our bags were part of that lively procession, being carried across the beach, down the float, and loaded aboard the vessel *Novo Nazare*.

THE RIO NEGRO

The Rio Negro is the only truly viable highway penetrating the remote wilderness of northern Brazil. This river not only dictates travel, it shapes the landscape, the weather pattern, and defines all life here, human and otherwise. In its annual pulses from wet to dry season, the water level can fluctuate some fifty feet. At the height of the flood, whole islands disappear and the forest is inundated for thousands of square miles. AFFE's fishing seasons are also dictated by these cycles. In high water periods, all the fish, including the peacocks, are widely dispersed into the flooded forest and essentially become inaccessible. With the onset of the dry period, the water recedes, sending the fish back into the re-formed lagoons, lakes, and channels,

Opposite page:
Peacock Bass, Rio Negro,
Amazonas, Brazil

43

Opposite page:
Jacunda, Rio Negro,
Amazonas, Brazil

where they remain until the next flooding season. At the height of the dry season, the main stem of the Rio Negro can become too shallow to navigate by river boat from Manaus to the prime fishing areas some 350 miles upstream. AFFE therefore fishes on either side of the extreme dry period, from August to early October, as the waters are in recession, then again from January to late February, just as they begin to rise again. In fact, the signs of this massive fluctuation are obvious any time we are close enough to see the trees on the banks, as they all have the telltale water marks high up on their trunks demarking where the water was and will be again in little more than a month.

AMAZON JUNGLE CRITTERS

After a few hours of steaming, we approached the Anavilhanas, the world's largest freshwater archipelago, comprising more than four hundred islands, some of which at this time of year are no more than huge, brilliant-white sandbars shimmering in stark contrast to the dark waters of the Negro. We made a brief stop at Novo Airao, the last village connected to Manaus by road, picked up a couple of skiffs, and then left civilization behind. This was also our literal jumping off point to the total Amazon immersion experience, as the crew beached the *Novo Nazare* on one of these islands and Octavio informed us we had stopped for a swim—just to cool off. "My wife's gonna kill me if she finds out I went swimming in the Amazon!" said Nick, and while no one commented, I know we were all thinking, "You go first, and if you do, she probably won't have to kill you." After all, everyone's heard the multitude of excruciating ways you can be killed, maimed, eaten, or infected by everything from insects to giant anacondas in the Amazon, right? Well, here it was, firsthand.

Even before getting our feet wet, let's deal with the issue of mosquitoes, malaria, and yellow fever. Mosquitoes do carry and transmit these diseases in Brazil and of course in some parts of the Amazon. However, because mosquitoes cannot breed in the acidic black-water sections of this river, they are virtually nonexistent in the Rio Negro, Scout's honor. Neither DEET nor nets are required. We didn't believe it either, and while most of us were taking anti-malaria meds (which are another tale in themselves), collectively, we probably got fewer than ten mosquito bites over the entire trip. The infamous piranha are indeed plentiful here, and we often saw the locals in small canoes fishing for them. We caught a fair number ourselves, and the worst thing they did was to shred flies or shear off leaders. They do have teeth like razors, and are aggressive and plentiful, but being reduced to bones by a ravenous horde of them only happens in the movies. Caiman, or *yacaré*, the South American crocodile, were a minor concern, and Tom and I were stopped one day from trying to swim to the far shore for worry there could be a few lurking over

there. Freshwater stingrays were a real concern, so when swimming or wading, we were advised to shuffle our feet in the sand to scare them off, just as you would wading a tropical saltwater flat. Problem solved. Finally, Octavio assured us that the big daddy of them all, the candiro, was not found in this part of the Amazon. Since he'd been right about the mosquitoes, we believed him about the rest, took the leap of faith, and neither surgery nor Cipro was required. And, as far as I know Nick's wife hasn't killed him yet either. From that moment forward, we were constantly in and out of the water, and despite the gallons of the bottled stuff we drank, our frequent dips were truly the only remedy for the heat.

What's a candiro, you ask? Well, hang on to your seat cushion. A candiro is a tiny catfish that is the only known vertebrate to parasitize humans. This tiny fish is fabled to have the ability to detect and swim up a urine stream, and the horrific habit of then lodging itself in the urethra in order to feed on blood and whatever else it might find there. In actual fact their upstream swimming abilities are highly exaggerated, but apparently they can indeed follow a urine trail and could potentially get into you if you urinate while swimming. While submerged, your next closest bodily orifice (and your belly button doesn't count) is also a prime target for a candiro invasion. While that seems punishment enough for even the most heinous pool pee-er, once lodged and feeding in this fashion, the candiro grows and swells. Only two remedies are known: surgical removal (not excluding amputation, if applicable), or stuffing the leaves of two specific medicinal plants in the orifice, which has the combined effect of killing and dissolving the offending party. The simplest cure, of course, is just to shoot yourself. Truth or jungle myth? Luckily, we never found out.

The Journey Upstream

For two full days we pushed upstream, through the ever narrowing, living walls of the jungle composed of untold thousands of species of plants, and a million shades of green. The vessel traffic common around Manaus had long since vanished, as well as most other signs of human interference. Periodically, we met commercial fishermen traveling in small riverboats, usually towing a string of small wooden dugout canoes behind. Most came alongside and were given some kind of supply while both crews chattered incomprehensibly to each other in river Portuguese and the fishermen furtively checked us out as if we were from another dimension. Through our entire upstream journey of over three hundred miles, we navigated through only one rocky narrows, for which we had to engage the services of a local pilot to make safe passage. Being on the tail end of the dry, low-water season, we often felt the *Novo Nazare* bump and slide over submerged sandbars. Even in stretches still a mile wide, a skiff was sometimes sent ahead to sound the depths with a stick to find the deep

Opposite page: Tararia, Rio Negro, Amazonas, Brazil

47

channels, but we still ran aground several times, each time watching with great anticipation as the propeller kicked up the pale sand off the bottom into the black water, making the prop-wash off the stern look like a huge cup of coffee into which we were stirring cream. We also managed on one such occasion to hit what must have been the only rock in the Rio Negro, which was particularly worrying, as it necessitated an impromptu inspection and repair of the prop and drive gear in a place where the prospects of being stranded were less than appealing.

Despite the rough spots, a leisurely and exotic if somewhat rustic cruise-ship ambience developed up on the top deck, which served as both lounge and sleeping quarters for the next two weeks. Here we luxuriated in the warm equatorial breezes and sipped cool drinks, tied leaders and flies, and otherwise fiddled with gear, read books, sunbathed, and of course asked a million and one stupid questions about life in the Amazon. After all, in this part of the world, asking seemingly stupid questions like, "Is it safe to pee in the river?" can have real survival value. Along those lines, within moments of taking our first tentative and awkward swings in our newly assigned hammocks, someone asked, "How do you screw in one of these?" Although a detailed explanation was never offered, as the nights passed it became painfully apparent that "How do you sleep in one," was by far the more relevant question concerning these outwardly graceful yet diabolically torturous cloth cocoons.

The days and nights, however, were full of wonder, as the jungle seemed to take on an increasingly primordial quality the farther we went and the remoteness of our position and ultimate destination began to have an impact you just cannot get from flying over such regions in an airplane. Here the only things flying were the small green parrots that flapped their way over the jungle canopy in the late afternoons, almost always in pairs, while through the days multitudes of other exotic birds like the toucan (the Fruit Loops bird) and the big, brightly colored macaws animated the treetops. We spotted the occasional caiman, otter, and bubblegum dolphin in the water, and were always on the lookout for monkeys and jaguars. Unfortunately, neither was sighted. Every couple of hours a plate of salami would appear from below decks, wonderful when eaten with fresh-squeezed lime. Other times, we'd get boiled and salted *pupunha*, the starchy little fruit of the peach palm. They're bright orange and taste something like a cross between a chestnut and a squash, somewhat bland but strangely addictive.

During this time we also become increasingly well acquainted with Octavio's partner, Mané, and the rest of the Brazilian crew: Ribamar, Djalmo, Marcello, and Rosario. As Octavio is the only one who speaks English, we taxed his patience and interpretive skills to the limit, and bridged the remaining gaps with a combination of charades and the creative linguistic talents of Tom and Lisa, as they attempted to go from English to Spanish to Portuguese and back again. Damn lucky we were only there fishing and not negotiating a treaty, but some things did start to become fairly clear. First, the only thing running through Mané's veins besides coffee, sugar, and nicotine is an intense passion for adventure angling. Several years before starting AFFE he explored much of Brazil's wilderness angling on his own and, obviously, his appetite for it has remained undiminished. His energy, drive, and enthusiasm were infectious. We also got our first hints that Riba (pronounced "Hiba" and short for Ribamar), is quite possibly Brazil's undiscovered answer to Crocodile Dundee. Because of the language barrier, most of what we had to go on were Riba's actions, but following him into the pitch-black of our first night on the river and watching him gleefully leave the boat to climb precariously over the water on the mangroves and grab a baby caiman with his bare hands was kind of a clue.

Virgin Backwaters

Finally, some 350 miles from Manaus, we reached the remote village of Vista Alegre, a small Caboclos outpost of about one hundred residents, and picked up our local guides, Oduan, Miguel, and, of course, Airuma. Beyond this point lies a confusing maze of waterways around a remote feeder tributary where AFFE is granted exclusive sport-fishing access, thanks to agreements with the government and local authorities. These were the unfished

Opposite page:
Piranha, Rio Negro,
Amazonas, Brazil

49

Opposite page:
Rio Negro, Amazonas, Brazil

waters Octavio had referred to in his e-mail, and we would spend the next week fishing far into these virgin backwaters. When water levels allow, the mother ship continues some forty miles further into this backcountry, but in our case low water had rendered this impossible. The *Novo Nazare* was therefore beached just downstream from the village, and from this home base, we set out each day in the skiffs. While the fishing in the vicinity of Vista Allegre itself was outstanding, Octavio and Mané insisted that it was better upstream, and so after taking a quick vote, our expedition-style fishing trip turned into its own little episode of *Survivor Amazon*, as we decided to venture upstream and spend a few nights camped in the jungle.

So, the next morning, we set out with three skiffs stuffed with gear and provisions on a three-hour cruise upstream to position ourselves in the middle of virgin waters. Our camp was set right at the jungle's edge on a beautiful white sand beach in an Eden-like setting. Logs cut from the forest and pounded into the sand by hand unbelievably formed a frame sturdy enough to hold all nine hammocks, and this frame was partially covered by a large blue tarp. We started out with this structure, a small table with benches, and a fire pit with a cooking rack, all of which was constructed from materials hacked out of the jungle and lashed together with bark and vines. Riba continually made improvements to the amenities, though, eventually adding a rod rack and a full-size bench complete with back rest, again using nothing more than a machete and his own ingenuity.

He even did some landscaping, cutting down some small palms and replanting them on the beach next to our fire pit, merely for aesthetic value. The whole place had a distinct Gilligan's Island flavor and indeed, given a few more days, I'm sure Riba would have built a dishwasher out of sticks and vines.

From this base we set out on daily missions exploring all the watery nooks and crannies of our private primordial paradise with the intent of picking fights with big peacocks every step of the way. No slough, channel, lagoon, or landlocked lake was spared from our sorties, as even overland travel with the skiff was not nearly enough to dissuade our stalwart guides from waters they deemed worthy for us to fish. When dry land got in the way, they simply employed the technique Octavio jokingly referred to as the "Amazon railway," whereby we became the porters, emptying the boat and carrying all the gear and equipment to the next put-in. Meanwhile, the guide, in our case Airuma, would build the railway by hacking down a couple of small trees, sectioning them into rollers, and laying them out crossways like railway ties ahead of the boat. We would then pull, push, and shove the boat over them until we ran out of rollers. Then, we'd walk back, retrieve the rollers, set them back out in front of the boat, and repeat the process until our destination waters were achieved. In the equatorial heat, I found the only way to endure the rigors of railway work was to rhythmically repeat Octavio's promise to myself in a mantra: "The rewards are usually worth anything, the rewards are usually worth anything." In his defense, usually they were.

Generally, fishing here involved working the shore-lines and shallows with blind casts primarily from the skiff, but also from our feet. Casting to peacocks chasing bait provided the most excitement, but we also had many opportunities to sight-cast to "laid-up" fish clearly visible in the shallows, which provided all of the attendant pleasures of that kind of fishing. Still other times, we cast to fish that only Airuma saw. How he saw them no one will ever know and, in fact, that he saw any fish at all seemed a miracle in itself, as he always sat low and cross-legged in the stern, slowly working the paddle. In addition, neither the blazing rays of the sun nor the huge flies that zipped around his head all day long could persuade him to put on polarized sunglasses. Despite all this, he periodically directed our casts away from the bank and other likely places and into mid-channel for no apparent reason, resulting in hookups with uncanny consistency. It was like fishing with Yoda.

The fishing situations and the species available varied widely and the angling was spectacular. Both butterfly and spotted peacocks occur here in sizes ranging from just a few pounds to near twenty, the largest one of our trip. Twenty peacocks per day averaging ten to twelve pounds was normal, interspersed by frequent catches of piranha, bicuda, jacunda, and traira. In fact very early in the trip it got to the point where Nick,

Lisa, and I began fishing flats-boat style—one angler at a time casting from the bow. Even at that, we often argued more from fatigue than politeness over whose turn it was to fish, each of us often insisting it was someone else's turn. In addition to the numbers of fish we caught, blind-casting a ten-weight in this heat was often brutally hard work.

The velvety warm jungle nights spent at camp were absolutely magical endings to perfect days. Here in the southern hemisphere, even the celestial ceiling is exotic, and while we could all point to Orion, we spent a good deal of time debating which of the jillion other stars formed the Southern Cross. Back on earth, scanning the opposite shore with flashlights revealed more ominous constellations formed by the distinctive dots of fiery orange eyeshine reflecting back from the cold reptilian peepers of the considerable local caiman population. In addition to the portable CD player we'd packed in, the insects, frogs, and howler monkeys filled the night air with what can only be described as a cacophony of cool jungle noises, just like in the movies, but occasionally supplemented by the peculiar cough-like bark of a jaguar. For those animals we didn't hear, Airuma needed no encouragement to oblige us with his impressions, each time sending everyone including himself into fits of hysterical laughter. With dinners of fresh peacock bass, chicken, and sausages roasted over an open fire, accompanied by Mané's delicious creations and a good supply of Chilean wine, Brazilian beer, local Pinga, and Scottish single malt whiskey, we had absolutely no reason to leave—except for running out of ice.

But since ice and time wait for no man, all too soon we were back on the *Novo Nazare*, retracing our route back downstream to Manaus. Like any homeward journey, let alone one from an Eden-like existence, it was a let-down, in this case tempered by the delight and comfort found in newly forged friendships and plans of future fishing adventures together. As you might expect, Octavio and Mané have no shortage of ideas in this respect, and after experiencing their expertise in these ventures, none of us would hesitate to go along. Octavio did finally reveal one of their secrets near the end of our trip, when he fessed up about Ariuma. "You know, his real name is Vivaldo. We just call him the Airuma." From his explanation, it seems the phenomenon of the Airuma or "Saci-Perere" is something like an Amazonian equivalent to a leprechaun and well known to all Brazilians. He is fabled to be a small black-skinned boy with only one leg who is continually playing mischievous tricks. Catch an Airuma, however, and he grants you your wishes in return for his freedom. So with this explanation, the great success of our trip, his prowess and antics in the jungle, and his uncanny ability to see invisible fish, all became clear.

The rainy season was working its way north and our southward re-entry to the Manaus area and civilization was marked by the first rains we'd seen in two weeks, coming appropriately on cue to wake us from the jungle dream we'd lived over the past fortnight. Like the fishing, there was little subtlety in the downpours, which were of a magnitude great enough to shock even a native of the Pacific Northwest. Throughout Brazil, the locals were gearing up for Carnival in a series of warm-up parties, and Lisa and I spent our last night in Manaus in the midst of one, enveloped in a sultry crush amid a sea of delirious, gyrating humanity packed like happy sardines into the plaza in front of the *Teatro Amazonas*. It seemed somehow fitting that this venerable symbol of excessive behavior could still summon it up from time to time, and seemed an equally fitting way to end our exotic and out-of-this-world Brazilian adventure.

CHAPTER 4

Russian Chrome
Steelhead: Kamchatka, Russia

"Where you go? No, no rest! You come, fish here, now!"

Though it was barked out in a thick, authoritarian Russian accent, absolutely nothing about this order was lost in the translation. I was definitely not taking a break, as intended. Instead, I was going to drag my arm-weary body back upstream and make what seemed like cast number 10,125 into a Russian steelhead stream—and now! After almost four days of waving my single-handed eight-weight with a sinking-tip line and a big weighted fly, I really was ready to take a breather, especially as thus far in my Russian steelheading career, I'd gone fishless. Blank. I was getting skunked and was worn out, to say the least.

Our guide, Vladimir Plotnikov, or Valodia, however, was having none of it. And although his accent and sometimes stern manner made all this a bit unsettling, Valodia was just displaying that quality common

to all great fishing guides everywhere. That is, he had an overwhelming desire to have his sport catch a fish. He knew the water was good and the fish were there, and took it almost personally if you didn't catch them. We've all experienced this before, but Valodia also had another pressing and perhaps more important reason I should catch a fish. Like all the guides here, he was pulling double duty as a fisheries biologist, and he wanted data.

In fact each and every sport-caught steelhead here yields not only a great story and photo for an angler, but valuable information in the form of scale samples, size, sex, and migration details, and is a vital part in an ongoing research and conservation project orchestrated by our hosts, the Wild Salmon Center, of Portland, Oregon. This study, which features a brilliant marriage between adventure angling and real ichthyological data-gathering, is indeed the only reason we are able to fish for steelhead in Russia in the first place, as they are

Ukhtolok River, Kamchatka, Russia

threw yet another tired, loose, ugly loop at the tundra clumps on the opposite bank and followed, yet again, the slow swing of my fly in what seemed to be a hardly flowing tundra stream as it meandered its way ever so patiently westward toward the Sea of Okhotsk.

The Sea of Okhotsk? Trying to say that is more like forcing a sneeze than naming the oceanic home of a sea-going rainbow. I mean, back home in British Columbia, steelhead run to the Pacific and return to rivers like the Dean, Thompson, Bulkley, and Babine—names that roll easily off the tongues of the devoted in an almost holy mantra in the cult of steelheading. The names of these Russian steelhead rivers I had only recently learned and still can't even properly pronounce, so while I was excited by the prospects of Russian angling, leaving British Columbia for steelhead felt a bit like leaving the state of Georgia in search of the perfect peach. That, however, was just the beginning.

It was 5:00 a.m. Friday morning. Following the red-eye flight from Seattle, I was in an airport seat opposite the Magadan Airlines counter in Anchorage, awaiting the once-weekly flight to Russia. Even before the dawn's early light, other rod tubes began to filter in, and from the initial, bleary-eyed, predawn murmurs, it was quite obvious that this wasn't just another fishing trip to one of the world's premier, heavily visited angling destinations. First off, no one else could say the names of the rivers they were going to either, and neither did anyone seem to know really what to expect

classified here as an endangered and protected species. So here in Russia, I had the unique opportunity to be a lousy angler and a worthless field researcher all at the same time, and I was taking full advantage of it.

I understood Vlad's frustration completely, as well as his good intentions, although frankly, a lot about this Russian steelheading was taking some getting used to. Even outside the research angle, it's all a bit different over here. But whatever the case, getting skunked was getting really old, and not wanting to annoy my new Russian friend any further, I tried to regain focus and waded my weary, sorry butt back out into the water and of the fishing. There was little of the educated antici-pation of a return visit in this crowd, but a lot more rumor and speculation in its place—the perfect start for a true angling adventure.

KAMCHATKA PENINSULA

Our destination city of Petropavlosk Kamchatsky was named by Vitus Bering for his two ships, the *St. Peter* and *St. Paul*, upon which he and legendary naturalist Georg Steller were sent from this very port by Catherine the Great in 1741 to go forth and discover an Alaska that no one really knew existed then. Just imagine your boss giving you a task like that: "Don't come back until you've found Alaska!" And in fact, Bering never did—come back, that is. Steller, on the other hand, not only came back, but apparently warmed up for this epic quest by first describing much of the flora and fauna of Kamchatka itself, among them, five species of Pacific salmon as well as the rainbow trout and steelhead and named them following the vernacular of the native Koryak people. These species names—*tshawytscha* (chinook salmon), *gorbuscha* (pink salmon), *nerka* (sockeye salmon), *keta* (chum salmon), *kisutch* (coho salmon), and of course *mykiss* (rainbow/steelhead)—are those we still use today. Okay, so maybe going to Kamchatka for steelhead wasn't so strange after all.

Not strange at all is more like it. The rivers drain-ing this thousand-mile-long peninsula flow into the Pacific, the Bering Sea, and the Sea of Okhotsk, making this the world's greatest salmonid motherlode, thought to account for up to one-third of the earth's entire popu-lation of these magnificent fish. Indeed, all six species of Pacific salmon occur here (the Asian masu salmon is the sixth), as well as four species of char, including the dis-tinctive white spotted char, or kundsha. Furthermore, as one of the last true remaining wild places on earth, much of this salmonid fishery remains pristine, representing not only an angler's paradise, but also a truly unique situation and a living laboratory for salmonid research and conservation that, without understatement, carries global implications.

Mi8 Helicopter, Kamchatka, Russia

57

For a salmonid snob from British Columbia, all this was a little hard to handle and maybe even a bit humbling. So, as it was for Steller, Kamchatka for me also represented a gateway to discovery. Ironically, my new vision here would be to see the world as it once was, to stand in streams that had followed only nature's course since even before Steller himself first cataloged their inhabitants for science. On the flip side, the initiatives of the Wild Salmon Center here offer a glimpse into the future of salmonid conservation, not only here but wherever the fish occur.

Simply put, post-Soviet Russia cannot yet afford to fund salmonid research in Kamchatka to the level that it deserves. As an economically developing nation, it still has way bigger fish to fry, so to speak. American anglers and their counterparts from other developed western nations, however, can afford such research. At the root of the Kamchatka Steelhead Project, it's as simple as that—internationally sponsored anglers financially enabling and participating in field-data gathering that otherwise would not get compiled. And yet, this is just the thin end of the wedge. Working from this basis, the folks at the Wild Salmon Center have created international collaborations both economic and academic and are talking about conservation models with timelines stretching thousands of years into the future with the vision of creating salmonid refuges throughout their range in perpetuity.

Kamchatka offered a unique situation to start. "It

59

[the resource] basically has one owner, it is intact with fish populations at historic levels, and there were few if any human alterations to the habitat," says Pete Soverel, Director of the Wild Salmon Center. "It's a place where you can see an end product to the conservation effort, and where we can really make a difference. The anglers are contributing to something that's truly achievable." In conservation terms, the brilliance in this strategy also lies in its creation of a number of directly interested constituencies (read motivated advocates), with international anglers, international academics, and everyone

Kvacina River Camp,
Kamchatka, Russia

Opposite page:
Snatolvayam River,
Kamchatka, Russia

Interior of tent. Kvacina
River Camp, Kamchatka,
Russia

Opposite page:
Russian Staff, Kvacina River
Camp, Kamchatka, Russia

60

else who benefits from tourism being the three most obvious. In this way, the center's conservation style is not just a pitch for the romantic concept of preserving something, in this case the world's greatest wild salmon runs, just for its inherent value. While that should be good enough, in reality it never is, and this program astutely recognizes that fact. Pete's vision of salmonid refuges doesn't mean creating places "where nothing else happens," but places where "source to mouth, salmon come first." Period.

The flight northwest from Petropavlosk Kamchatsky to steelhead central in the classic and infamous Russian MI-8 helicopter was nothing short of astounding. Our first astonishment—that the flight was actually achieved—was quickly replaced by the thrill of the breathtaking and exotic vistas that opened up below as we flew across and up the peninsula through dizzying mountain passes surrounded by stunning volcanic peaks and over expansive birch forests that finally gave way to open, rolling grasslands and tundra. We made one refueling stop at the halfway point in a small hamlet, which curiously enough is named Esso, and resumed our flight toward the promised land.

THE KVACINA RIVER CAMP

After about an hour-long flight from Esso, we saw the sinuous Kvacina River twisting its way through the rolling tundra below us toward the incongruously

jagged peaks of Cape Uktolok jutting up from the sea like a small, isolated mountain range to the west. From aloft, the bright orange tents of our camp looked like a cluster of huge, otherworldly mushrooms growing out of the boggy tundra. From the ground, it was apparent that this was as much a field biology camp as it was a fishing camp, with "camp" being the operative word in both cases; comfortable, adequate, and safe, but let's just say that a full-service spa and white linen tablecloths aren't likely to be added to the operation any time soon. Having said that, the makeshift streamside *banya*, a combination shower/sauna heated by a woodstove, was truly a warm, steamy oasis of pure luxury in the heart of the Kamchatkan wilderness and more than made up for any lack of more conventional creature comforts.

The camp is run by a local operator contracted by the Wild Salmon River Expeditions, and the staff is entirely Russian, except for Dave Goodhart, an American acting as co-camp manager, head guide, and liaison between us and the staff. Everyone except Dave was a bit shy, but everyone including Dave was warm, friendly, and accommodating. We quickly and easily slipped across the language and culture barrier into a comfortable and pleasant daily routine, with our guides, Alexander Polunin, or Sasha, and Valodia acting as our main interpreters, and Russian vodka as our main lubricant. We were soon using the standard Russian words for "good morning" (*dobray ootra*), "thank you" (*spasiba*), and "you're welcome" (*pazhalusta*), and learned

63

many more colorful words and phrases which would be useful anywhere and anytime, whether fishing was involved or not.

Meals were taken in the cook shack, the only wooden structure in the entire camp (besides the outhouse), and starvation was never a concern. At any time of the day, plates of cookies and salami were kept on the table, alongside an exotic array of condiments ranging from hot sauce to chocolate spread. Rasputin himself leered back at us from his prominent position on the mustard bottles, which also featured other figures from Russian history, all of whom curiously appeared

Russian guide, Kvacina River Camp, Kamchatka, Russia

Opposite page:
Kvacina River, Kamchatka, Russia

Steelhead, Kvacina River,
Kamchatka, Russia

Opposite page:
Steelhead, Kvacina River,
Kamchatka, Russia

camp cuisine even remotely unpalatable. And best of all, cans of Baltika 4, a really good Russian beer, and small bottles of vodka about the same size as the beer cans never seemed to be in short supply.

The sleeping arrangements were two to a tent, each equipped with two cots, two chairs, one small table, ample room for all our gear, and a central woodstove that often seemed like it could keep all of hell itself at its required temperature. This intense heat was always preceded by a visit from our new friend Pasha and his trusty bottle of kerosene. Like a kind of fire fairy, every evening just after dinner he would visit each tent and crank up the stove. Early each morning, before we awoke, he would return to breathe fire into the stoves yet again, and while stepping out of a warm sleeping bag into a comfortably heated tent was indeed a luxury, if you didn't do it within fifteen minutes of his visit, you were in grave danger of sweating yourself skinny. "Pasha the Dragon," as we came to call him, did keep it violently hot, so I'm half expecting to find his mug featured on a Russian mustard bottle sometime soon.

From this camp, we fished both the Kvacina and Snatolvayam Rivers, which meet at a common estuary. Unlike the raucous and rocky western North American rivers that I normally associate with steelhead, these rivers are by comparison tranquil and serene, and while they run through exceedingly picturesque settings, they seem a bit like, well, drainage ditches. They are both low-gradient streams with clay banks and muddy

to share a notorious and violent quality in the scenes depicted on the otherwise ordinary yellow squeeze bottles. We named it "bad boy mustard" and never really understood how these guys helped increase mustard sales. We never really understood why the bacon was always served raw, either, but that was the only part of

bottoms, and clear but tannin-stained waters. Even single-handed, you can usually bounce your fly off the opposite bank fairly easily on either stream, and indeed in a lot of places you could throw twenty feet of fly line right up onto the opposite shore if you weren't paying attention. Gravel bars are scarce, and there is hardly a rock between these two rivers big enough for any self-respecting steelhead to sit behind. So what do they do? Mostly, they hug the cut banks or sit behind tundra clumps, which are exactly that—large clumps of muddy, clay-like tundra eroded from the bank. These rivers are real sleepers: The features and flow are subtle, wading is easy, and just by looking at them, you'd be hard pressed to believe that any steelhead would actually run up them.

Outward appearances proved deceiving, though. Shortly after our arrival and before anyone was even unpacked, let alone unwound, Paul and Mike were geared up and out on the water. And, in those short couple of hours before dusk, the little Kvacina River rewarded their initiative admirably by spitting out proof in the form of the largest steelhead of the trip. It was an absolute hog, a male over twenty pounds, measuring a full thirty-eight by twenty-one inches and Mike's first steelhead ever, immediately confirming that not only do big, fat steelhead run up this small, skinny stream, but also, that steelheading, whether Russian or otherwise, ain't always fair. This event, along with several shots of "welcome to Russia" vodka, had also convinced me that I had reached steelhead heaven without having died first, and in the giddy mindlessness of this epiphany, I momentarily forgot my abject fear of and ineptitude with horses and volunteered for a trip to the Snatolvayam the very next morning, a journey that required a horseback ride of about an hour. The "Snat" was described as even smaller than the Kvacina, yet known to hold even bigger fish.

THE SNATOLVAYAM

So, in the sober first light of day one in Russia I found myself surveying the boundless tundra from atop a smallish Asian horse upon which I was very uneasily perched. First the sketchy helicopter, and now this? But the onset of fall had transformed the low-lying tundra vegetation into a rolling sea of muted reds and golds and greens as far as the eye could see, and just five minutes from camp there was nothing but Kamchatka as God created it. The vistas addle your brain as it struggles to process the vast abundance of tranquil beauty that your eyes greedily funnel into it, and even at that you feel cheated that you can't spin your head like an owl. The rhythmic breathing and squishing of the horses' hooves sinking into the boggy tundra is all you hear, punctuated periodically by flocks of ptarmigan that flush from the grasses and fly away low before you. Dwarfed by the sheer scale of the land, you feel swallowed up and puny, and the sheer beauty of the surrounding landscape makes you feel like you're riding a flea across some impressionist's canvas. The horseback ride to the Snat is nothing short of sublime, and can even cure you of a fear of horses.

There were five anglers in our group, and over the next week, we took turns fishing both the Kvacina and the Snatolvayam where a total of thirty-six fish were caught: twenty-three males and thirteen females. Since the fishing here was either in water influenced by tides or nearly so, all the fish caught were chrome-bright and shaped like footballs, and as a group, they were noticeably fatter than most other steelhead I've seen. One day was lost on the Kvacina due to heavy rain and a blown-out river, but the Snatolvayam still managed to produce two fish that day. Over the course of the week, Mike and Jim each had a spectacular five-fish day, Mike's coming on the Snat, and Jim's on the Kvacina. Each fish landed was carefully measured, sexed, relieved of at least ten scales, adorned with a tag, and released unharmed. The data derived will eventually be assimilated into the next of an already considerable series of scientific papers that have already revealed a wealth of incredible secrets about salmonid life history.

THE UKHTOLOK RIVER

The Ukhtolok River and camp is about a half-hour helicopter flight southwest from the Kvacina camp, and this is where we spent our second week. A huge

Opposite page:
Kvacina River Camp,
Kamchatka, Russia

67

low-pressure system over the Sea of Okhotsk sent a typhoon tracking toward us, and although we were never subjected to the full brunt of its force, the mere edges of its fury bestowed howling winds and waves of torrential rain showers upon us, and the rivers quickly began to rise. The Kvacina was unfishable the day we left and remained that way for most of the following week. Unfortunately, the neighboring Uktholok suffered the same fate.

Wherever steelheaders congregate and aren't fishing, invariably the overwhelming majority of their conversations will revolve around two main topics: the exact definition of a steelhead and the finer points of fly casting. If you accept this as an immutable law of nature, Kamchatka is indeed the perfect place to be, as not only does it hold one-third of the world's salmonids, this week it also held an abundance of expertise on these two subjects in the form of Pete Soverel and Serge Karpovich, founders of the Wild Salmon Center, and Professor Oksana Savvaitova, grande dame of steelhead research from Moscow State University. In addition, two of the finest double-handed fly casters you are ever likely to meet in the form of Monte Ward and Ed Ward (no relation). The rest of us in camp rounded out the faculty.

So, over the course of the week, we had a steelhead school like no other, where everything you thought you knew about rainbows and steelhead got turned right on its ear and you watched guys cast fly lines farther than you ever thought possible. As far as the fish were concerned, research here has revealed more than nineteen different life histories for the rainbow/steelhead in Kamchatka. Some go to sea for varying intervals, some don't, and some do both by spending their first four or five years as resident, stream-dwelling rainbows and then become steelhead by adopting an anadromous lifestyle. (That's not something we generally accept as possible in North America.) A scale sample can not only tell you the age of its donor, it can reveal whether or not it went to sea, how often, and—get a load of this— whether its *mother* was a sea-going or resident fish! Its mother! Furthermore, it has been shown that resident fish can produce anadromous offspring and vice versa. Much of this information confounds generally accepted notions we hold about the rainbow/steelhead, and you don't have to be a fisheries biologist to recognize its value and significance for conservation.

When I did finally manage a scientific contribution of my own, it came on the Kvacina River and on that very cast that Vlad so gently persuaded me to make. The fish took just as my line straightened out and the fly had started its drift along the opposite shore. Luckily, it wasn't one of those tentative, tapping kind of steelhead takes, which might have required some skill and patience on my part, but thankfully was a no-brainer signaled by the unmistakable toilet-bowl flush and powerful tug from an obviously suicidal steelhead swirling decisively on my fly. I don't know who was happier at that moment, Vlad or me, but he definitely yelled louder: "Your first Russian steelhead!" Like all good steelhead, it showed me a fair bit of my backing and suspended time in a series of deliciously tense moments. Unlike most steelhead, this seventeen-pound male also gave up ten scales to the data pool and was tagged prior to release. But for me, that was it. I was to be a one-fish wonder in Kamchatka, which isn't exactly easy in the land that holds most of the world's salmon. But sometimes fishing's just like that. So despite the fact that I have to tell that to the world, I am taking solace in the fact that it was the only steelhead I've ever caught that was part of something truly bigger and with far more significance than just another fish. And, it was a fitting ending to an overall experience I wouldn't trade for a month of ten-fish days back home.

I have to admit that at first, being a born skeptic, I thought the science program here might be just a slick scheme for taking tax-deductible fishing trips. But I was as wrong about that as I was for thinking British Columbia was the sole center of the steelhead universe. I now know that there are at least two. And I know that if the Wild Salmon Center has anything to do with it, there will always be places like this, where anglers not only enjoy the resource but also help to ensure its healthy continuance.

As you might expect, Soverel e-mailed me upon his return home to inform me that a couple of days after our departure, the rivers dropped back into shape, and well, you know the rest—they hammered 'em. I mean, they collected lots of data. I believe him. There is one thing above all that's different about steelheading in Russia: You can't lie about it because it all gets scientifically documented.

CHAPTER 5

Days of Wine and Rises
Doves and Trout: Argentina

It's Tuesday, so this must be Buenos Aires. I know, that's an old cliché, and while only a true dunce could confuse this fabulous city for any other, I'd been on a bit of a wild run through Argentina for almost a week already, so this day, that's about all my weary brain could muster. And sure enough, speeding from the domestic *aeroparque* over to international terminal, Buenos Aires flashed by the taxicab window like a slide show on uppers while my mind chugged slowly along behind, still working on last week's events. Was I really back here already? What happened? Where was I going? Don't tell me I'm leaving already! But through my blissful if somewhat confused haze, one thing was clear. I was definitely not ready to leave. I needed more time here, lots more time. Luckily, I wasn't quite finished with Argentina just yet—but that's another story altogether.

Argentina. Just say that word to a fly fisherman and chances are, his eyes will glaze over. If he wing-shoots

as well, then his jaw will likely go slack too. Then, if you mention Malbec, he might even begin to drool. That's pretty much what happened to me at the beginning of all this anyway, and I can't be all that different from any other obsessive, fly-fishing, wing-shooting, wine-quaffing "fun-hog" (a label once attached to me by an editor) out there. After all, who among us hasn't fantasized about fishing the Traful, Chimehuin, Alumine, Rio Grande, or any of the countless other storied streams of this southern country? Similarly, who hasn't dreamt of days on doves, perdiz, Magellanic geese, or any of the other exotic southern birds for which Argentina is so rightfully renowned? Finally, in addition to all the sport, did you know that Argentina is also the fifth largest wine-producing nation in the world?

So when it was suggested that I trade the damp chill of late winter in the Pacific Northwest for the mellow warmth of late summer in the southern hemisphere, I'll readily

Opposite page:
Dove hunting, Cordoba,
Argentina

admit to a temporary loss of composure. "Hey man, why don't you go to Argentina," was how the phone call from my publisher began. And while I was all ears at this point, I didn't really hear quite what I had expected. Of the countless dream streams of this country that I'd spent so many hours fantasizing about, surprisingly, not even one was mentioned. Indeed, what was outlined wasn't really even a fishing trip—not exactly anyway.

"I want you to cover a cool trip that John Ecklund at Rivers to Reefs has put together in northern Argentina," the outline began. "Start in Buenos Aires, and then fly out to Cordoba for a couple of days on doves, then go across to Mendoza and tour a bunch of wineries, check out the wine scene, and then shoot down into northern Patagonia to spend a couple of days fishing somewhere in the Andes—don't know the names of the rivers but it sounds pretty cool, undiscovered. It's all arranged. You'll be totally looked after and you need to leave on March 22. Alicia's gonna send your tickets. I'll e-mail you the itinerary and if you have questions, you can contact John directly."

So there it was: undiscovered fishing in Patagonia with wing shooting and wine drinking to boot. Could it get any better than that? Well, perhaps. For once I examined my itinerary more closely, there were a few points about this little jaunt that gave me pause to consider. There was indeed some fishing involved, but it was limited to just two days at the tail-end of the season. And, although I've shot at a fair number of birds in my day and do truly love the sport, I wing-shoot like I golf, which means I spend most of my time spraying errant shots all over the place, invariably threatening far fewer birdies or birds than I'd really like. And the wine? Well, over the years, my relationship with wine has generally been a very happy and rewarding one. But an erudite oenophile I am not, so I wondered how I'd fare in a world where the pros can detect multilayered essences of exotic fruits and flavors and even be so inspired to assign multiple personality traits to old grape juice. But those were minor worries. My real concern was the schedule, which had obviously been set up by someone with a "sleep when you're dead" philosophy. But this was a run through Argentina after all, and with all that excitement in the offing, who could sleep anyway?

DOVES UNLIMITED

The City of Cordoba is slightly north of Buenos Aires about smack-dab in the center of the country. At latitude 31° south, it is roughly the same distance from the equator as San Diego, California. It is a historic and culturally important city, founded by Jesuits and second only in stature to the capital, Buenos Aires. Nestled in the Sierra Chico Mountains and bordered by rich farmland, Cordoba is also the undisputed dove-shooting mecca of the world. The climate, surrounding hills, and seemingly endless acres of cultivated grain fields make perfect dove habitat, and much to the

chagrin and detriment of the Argentinean agriculture industry, the dove population here numbers in the tens of millions. Every season in Cordoba, therefore, is open season on doves, and nowhere on earth is the term "high-volume wing-shooting" more appropriate. So although somewhat dulled by more than twenty-six hours in transit from Vancouver, and definitely in no shape to be swinging on anything with a shotgun, I arrived in Cordoba optimistic. With that many little grain thieves flying around, I figured even I was bound to hit quite a few, and looked forward to doing my little bit of pest control on behalf of the Argentinean farmer.

Robin Benedict, longtime general manager of David Denies's dove shooting operation, was at the airport to drive me out to the Pica Zuro Lodge. Along the way, he provided me with a brief but entertaining primer on Argentine political history from Peron to the present, and, of course, gave me the lowdown on the dove situation. As we chatted, small flocks of birds occasionally fluttered across the fields in the soft, early evening light, but in a place where doves are tallied in numbers more typical for swarms of insects, I had come here almost expecting them to be bouncing off the windshield like bugs. So where were all the doves? Robin explained that because of the season and the timing of the harvests, we were in a transitional period. This meant that the huge clouds of doves which can sometimes stream by for hours on end as they move from roost to field and back weren't quite happening right now, and, in fact, the best fields they

were shooting currently were a lot farther from the lodge than normal. The birds were still plentiful, of course, just not at their absolute peak.

A completely restored nineteenth-century hacienda, Pica Zuro Lodge is a luxurious yet casually elegant oasis situated on a working estancia. Guests are accommodated in eight spacious and fully appointed bedrooms situated around the core of the building, which includes a large, comfortable sitting room and adjacent dining room. High vaulted ceilings throughout create an airy, open atmosphere further emphasized by the traditional hacienda-style veranda surrounding the building. In addition, this facility also boasts a swimming pool, game room, and on-call masseuse. Could there be a more perfect setting to unwind in after flying almost halfway around the world? I didn't think so, and as luck would have it, I arrived here precisely at cocktail hour. Argentina was already looking pretty fine, and I hadn't really even done anything yet. Moreover, as the evening progressed, the outlook just kept getting brighter: cocktails, a spectacular gourmet meal of fine Argentinean beef accompanied with a rich, red Malbec, shooting stories from that afternoon, and the approaching promise of a little shut-eye.

At the 5:30 a.m. wake-up call, I barely felt like I'd blinked. In fact, I may not even have been fully awake as our shooting party of five, plus bird boys and guides, started spreading out along the fence line of a soybean field, because for a quick second, it looked to me like we were marching into some kind of a war. Filing back and forth from the vehicles like a procession of ants, our guides packed armfuls of shotguns and cases upon cases of *cartuchas* in preparation for the morning's events. And then, as if on cue, the doves began to fly. Initially, just a few birds ducked and dived through the nearby treetops, and the first tentative shots and cheers rang out down the line. As the morning progressed, the shooting became continuous, as wave upon wave of doves simply kept on coming and coming and coming. Granted, these weren't the dense, block-out-the-sun kind of flocks I'd expected, but it was a mind-blowing stream nonetheless. Groups of five and six, then flocks of fifty, then a hundred and fifty, and so on just kept coming out of nowhere as if someone had turned on a tap.

Dove shooting Cordoba-style was a lot more fun than I had imagined, and not just because of the volume of doves. For this lazy fun-hog, the best part was the almost complete lack of encumbrances involved; that is, there was no screwing around with decoys, dogs, camo, calls, waders, boats, or anything of the like. All you needed here was a shotgun or two and what seemed like enough ammo to topple a small West African dictatorship. Indeed the copious ammo requirement was the only glitch in this maximum fun for minimum work wing shooting, but luckily that detail was taken care of by an expert group of guides and bird boys.

In fact, in addition to the sheer numbers of birds, the work done by Pablo Aguilo and his able crew is really makes this experience special. Not only do they keep cases of ammo at your feet, they also act as loaders, ensuring your second double is always ready, or sitting beside you and pumping shells into your auto between shots. They help spot the incoming birds, offer valuable shooting advice, keep a tally of downed birds with hand counters, and then go and collect them all afterward. At lunch time they turn into chefs, preparing a delicious *asado*, or Argentinean barbecue, in the field, complete with dining tent, tablecloths, fine wine, and even hammocks strung in the shade for those who need to treat their aching shoulders and bulging stomachs to a little midday siesta. And in their spare moments, if you pass over the guns and insist, they'll show you how to really wreak havoc on doves.

I was infatuated with dove shooting early into the first day, and fully in love with it partway into the second. This day, the birds flew high and fast—confoundingly harder to hit, but all that much better when you did. And, coming on the heels of yet another evening of Pica Zuro hospitality, I was settling into this whole program nicely and even felt like I'd caught up on a bit of sleep. But just as I was getting comfortable, my schedule tapped me on the shoulder, and before I knew it, I was back at the Cordoba Airport. Next stop: Mendoza.

WINE COUNTRY

The wine and Patagonian trout fishing portion of my journey came with a peculiar warning. My scheduled

Mendoza, Argentina

76

tour guide was apparently something of a femme fatale, which is a noteworthy reputation to possess in a country often rumored to hold a disproportionate percentage of the world's most desirable women. "Apparently everyone falls in love with Jimena," were among the intriguing words my editor passed along well before I'd even left home. So, just try to imagine the utter depths of my disappointment when, upon arriving in Mendoza, I was met not by the storied Jimena, but instead by the never-before-mentioned Juan. Juan? Por favor! Surely someone had made a terrible mistake. But no such luck. Jimena had indeed been reassigned, and I wound up with Juan. Now don't get me wrong, ladies; Juan is a charismatic, strapping young Argentinean polo player who I'm sure any of you would be more than thrilled to know, but he was a far, far cry from what I was led to expect.

To his credit, however, Juan quickly proved to be indispensable. As an interpreter, he was an ace. Juan speaks better English than most North Americans I know, and even went so far as to restate for me things I'd been told by other English-speaking Argentinians. As a tour guide, he was enthusiastic. Juan was proud and passionate about this place and eager to show off all its considerable attributes. Finally, Juan was also dialed right in to all the exciting developments currently blossoming in the food and wine world of Mendoza, so my upcoming wine education was definitely in good hands. In short, he was almost the perfect host/interpreter/companion to steer me through the next four whirlwind days. But he was still no Jimena.

Argentina is one of the world's largest wine producers, with a venerable history of viniculture reaching back over 500 years, and at the very heart of it all is the beautiful city of Mendoza. I arrived here at the tail end of *vendimia*, the wine harvest, and the sweet smell of crushed fruit filled the taxi even as we drove from the airport into and throughout the city. Up until quite recently, almost all of Argentine wine was consumed domestically and was not considered export grade. Today, however, domestic consumption is down, quality and exports are up, and you barely have to be in Mendoza long enough to sip, swirl, and spit to see that Argentina's massive wine industry is on the brink of a boom. It seemed everyone here was planting vines, growing grapes, and building wineries, ranging from small, owner-operated, boutique-type bodegas right through to international heavyweights like Moët & Chandon, Cordoniu, and Lafite Rothschild. Mendoza was truly abuzz with wine, so to speak, and my schedule here was a mad charge to see (and drink) as much of it as humanly possible in the short time allotted.

In contrast to the wide-open landscapes of Cordoba, the vineyards of Mendoza are stuck right up against the towering, jagged and imposing edifice of the Andes. In fact, the province of Mendoza is home to Cerro Aconcagua, the highest peak in the western hemisphere, so it shouldn't come as any surprise that this region also holds some of the highest and most scenic vineyards in the world. Indeed, the various altitudes at which grapes are grown here is considered an important factor in determining their quality, giving the phrase "high on wine" a whole new meaning. I spent my first night on the grounds of the Terrazas de los Andes Winery, named for the various terraces upon which its grapes are grown, and where just fifty paces from my room at the *hosteria*, freshly picked grapes were being unloaded, sorted, and cleaned well into the night.

So, while still drunk on doves and fighting an ever-growing sleep deficit, my first morning in Argentina's

Bodega Catena Zapata, Mendoza, Argentina

city of wine was a blur of vineyards, grape crushers, stainless steel tanks, oak casks, and bottling lines as we sprinted through two major wineries before noon, pausing only to catch our breath in their luxuriously appointed and well stocked tasting rooms. Terrazas de los Andes and Salentein are both huge, multimillion-dollar facilities, and the product produced within them did indeed beckon for a more prolonged visit, but once again, my schedule forced a premature departure. We had a pressing appointment to keep, as we were to meet up with our fishing guide for lunch before embarking on the four-hour drive into northern Patagonia to fish.

Opposite page:
Rio Tordillo, Provincia
Mendoza, Argentina

TROUT IN VALLE HERMOSO

Despite our best efforts, Juan and I arrived at the Posada del Jamon with wine on our breath, a little bleary eyed, and a couple of hours late: a great way to make a good first impression. Like almost every other place I had visited so far, this charming, authentic little bistro-style restaurant in the heart of wine country deserved a much longer stay, but since we'd already kept our fishing hosts waiting, we quickly chucked down some chow and hit the road for Patagonia. It was a rather unlikely fishing foursome that took to the road this day. I was the non-Spanish speaking, Canadian angling vagrant posing as a photojournalist. And of course Juan, interpreter, host, and polo player par excellence but someone who had never fly-fished before in his life. Then there was our guide and driver, Fernando Mosso, an Argentinean squash champion, a certified, Mel Krieger fly-fishing instructor, full-time jokester, and amiable friend to all. Finally, there was Gustavo, angling companion to Fernando, new acquaintance to both me and Juan, and—last but not least—the lucky husband of none other than the legendary Jimena.

Despite our disparate interests, backgrounds, and a small language barrier, we laughed and joked like old friends as we bumped along the eastern edge of the Andes, four hundred kilometers south into Patagonia and the ski resort of Las Lenas. And, over the course of this four-hour trek, I was educated in some essential matters of Argentinean culture. First, I learned how to drink *maté*, and the associated points of etiquette to be observed while partaking of this ubiquitous and effective Argentinean stimulant. I also learned the legends of la Difunta Correa and Guachito Gil, two of the most revered folk saints of this country who are honored in thousands of conspicuous roadside shrines almost everywhere you go. And finally, through the dedicated and enthusiastic tutoring from my three new amigos, I leaned to swear in Spanish like an Argentinean longshoreman, language I quickly learned to apply in reference to—you got it—The Schedule.

For skiers, Las Lenas is one of Argentina's finest destinations, boasting a vertical drop of more than four thousand feet, a top elevation of more than twelve thousand feet, and more gnarly, off-trail descents than an old two-planker like me could shake a ski pole at. For anglers, it is the gateway to some of northern Patagonia's least known and most spectacularly scenic wilderness fishing for resident rainbows, browns, and brookies. Our plan for the next two days was to fish the river systems of the nearby Valle Hermoso, composed of the Rio Tordillo and Rio Cobre, which join to form the Rio Grande, and the Arroyo Las Cargas, a small, spring creek-like stream that joins the main river farther downstream.

The road into Valle Hermoso is a rough dirt four-wheel-drive track that leads through the ski area and over a mountain pass before plunging steeply into a twisting series of switchbacks. From the top of the pass,

Argentinean guide, Provincia Mendoza, Argentina

80

like terrain surrounded by imposingly jagged twelve-thousand foot peaks that look like they've been adorned with a multicolored watercolor wash of swirling earthy hues. The scenery here is nothing short of sublime, but as I gushed on about it, Fernando looked over with a knowing yet silly grin and said to Juan in Spanish, "Tell him this is the ugliest place we fish."

On this day, likely because it was the tail-end of the season and Valle Hermoso is known only to Argentinos, we had the place to ourselves. And while Fernando had warned that this wasn't exactly prime time, he was hooked up before the rest of us even had our waders on to a beautiful and extraordinarily fat, healthy-looking, three-pound rainbow. For the balance of the day, we fished on foot—up the Rio Tordillo, back down to the Rio Cobre confluence, and partway down the Rio Grande. In this region, all three rivers are medium to small freestone streams that can be crossed fairly easily at certain points. All include a classic series of riffles, runs, pockets, and pools, with enough big boulders strewn in to make for really interesting water. And, despite what Fernando might tell you, in the Valle Hermoso the true challenge is to keep focused on fishing, rather than just spending your day looking up and gawking at all the incredible scenery.

The same day, the Rio Tordillo produced fairly consistently, giving up several rainbows ranging from one-and-a-half to three pounds, all on nymphs fished upstream with zero- to three-weight rods. Downstream

the vistas down into the valley and west to the high peaks of the Andes are the most stunning alpine views I've ever seen. From here, you can clearly see the confluence of the Rio Tordillo and Rio Cobre as they wind their way through an austere, treeless, moonscape-

of the confluence with the Rio Cobre, in the slightly bigger water of the Rio Grande, brown trout of about the same size were the prevalent species. Fernando assured me that fish in the over five-pound category were also possible, as well as great dry-fly fishing in season, and he had plenty of proof on his digital camera to back up his claim. Some of these photos, Fernando explained, were of fish caught during extended horseback trips he leads into the more remote regions of the upper Rio Tordillo. Considering the scenery and the absolute hog rainbows in the photographs, even this confirmed horse hater could have easily been convinced to mount up and head into those hills.

On day two, we set off from Las Lenas for Arroyo Las Cargas. It was a slightly longer drive through equally spectacular scenery, but the really interesting part of this little trip came as it appeared we were about to cross a fairly wide lower section of the Rio Grande in the Land Rover. Not far downstream from this spot, the river gathered into a steep, heavy rapid that might have been feasible in a rubber raft, but visions of tumbling through it while strapped into a Land Rover were somewhat less than appealing. Feigning as much nonchalance as possible, I appealed to Juan: "Can you ask Fernando if we're really gonna cross here? Like, in the truck?" I know Juan asked the question, as he appeared equally surprised by the events that were about to unfold. In response, Fernando eased the vehicle into the current, and with a huge, relaxed grin, said

what basically translated into, "Yeah, we do this all the time," while coaxing the Land Rover in well past its wheel wells. Maybe so, but that was little comfort as I nervously watched the water pile up on our upstream side right to the bottom of the windows and felt the rather unnerving sensation of the vehicle being shoved sideways, quartering downstream, as we half drove, half bobbed our way across the Rio Grande.

And the fun wasn't over yet, for the rest of the rocky road into Las Cargas seemed little more than a slightly widened goat trail with a precipitous drop on the downhill side. Quite incredibly, it was built by Fernando and

Rainbow trout, Rio Tordillo, Provincia Mendoza, Argentina

81

his buddies, all by hand and one rock at a time. Fernando explained that he had been granted an exclusive right from the government to operate as a fishing guide in Las Cargas, so in addition to clearing this track, they had also made other sweat-equity investments here. Among other things, they had started to build a small stone lodge in this valley, and some time ago, Fernando had made an initial planting of one thousand rainbows and three hundred brook trout. When we reached the end of the track, the valley proper was still a four-kilometer hike away along a steep and even narrower side-hill track that followed the lower course of the river.

In contrast to the classic freestone character of the Rio Tordillo/Cobre system, Las Cargas has the serene ambience of a tiny spring creek, with still, glassy glides, undercut banks, and thick patches of weeds. This braided, meandering little creek seems to flow from as far upstream as the eye can see, and its beauty is amplified by the somewhat incongruous setting, as it flows though the center of a huge alpine valley surrounded on both sides by the impossibly tall, jagged, and anything but peaceful-looking peaks of the Andes. From here, Chile is less than 10 kilometers away. Being completely unaccustomed to fishing spring creeks and tiny streams in general, I spent most of the morning wandering several kilometers upstream, unwittingly walking past most of the productive pockets and undercuts, which to my untrained eye looked too puny to hold anything but the odd little frog. Whenever I did cast, however,

I almost always hooked a bright, beautiful little ten- to twelve-inch brookie, or *fontinalis*, as they call them there. Whatever you call them, they were everywhere.

Then, about halfway through our fishing day, as Fernando and I began searching for bigger rainbows in all the good water I'd missed, the weather gods rudely intervened. After what had started out as an idyllic, blue-bird day, menacing clouds gathered over the mountains and powerful gusts of wind boomed down the valley, pushed ahead by a series of violent squalls rapidly blowing in from the west. The skies darkened quickly, huge dust devils danced in and around the surrounding peaks, and the scene suddenly turned from majestically serene to majestically scary. Blown out of Las Cargas by a powerful mountain storm, we were forced to beat a hasty retreat back down our goat trail to the Land Rover.

In an equally unexpected development, we reached the Rio Grande crossing once again only to find some *puesteros*, the semi-nomadic ranchers found in this region, busily herding up their goats, sheep, and horses and throwing them in the back of large open trucks in order to move them out of the high country for the winter. Considering the impending storm, we decided to stay awhile and lend a hand in the roundup, participating in what might kindly be called a crazy, impromptu little rodeo. As it unfolded, this spectacle became more like a cross between a rugby match and a roundup: the Patagonian sheep and goats squad with home field advantage versus the *puesteros* and visiting

anglers. Our strategy was simple. Sheep were herded toward the river, and once within range, the idea was to jump the herd in unison, grab as many as possible, and throw them into the trucks. In the execution, only a few sheep actually fell for this ploy on any given drive. The rest just exploded away in all directions—running, kicking, and jumping, often dragging a *puestero* or wader-

Puesteros, Provincia Mendoza, Argentina

Opposite page: Arroyo Las Cargas, Provincia Mendoza, Argentina

clad angler behind. It was a spontaneous and hilarious two hours, which made us forget the disappointment of our foreshortened fishing day, and while it was the only event not previously dictated by The Schedule, it was easily as entertaining as everything that was.

We left Las Lenas at sunrise the following morning, with new snow from the previous day's storm shimmering off the surrounding peaks. Still slaves to our uncompromising and relentless timetable, today would bring a four-hour drive back to Mendoza and directly into wine, wine, and then more wine. First, an exhaustive tour and lunch appointment at the impressive Septima Winery, the Argentinean arm of the Spanish Cordoniu Group. From there we proceeded directly to Dolium, a small boutique winery that is unique in being built entirely underground to ensure temperature consistency. The owner himself, Mario Giadorou, an engineer by profession, proudly gave us a tour through his facility, a testament to one man's devotion to the art of wine making. Finally, to finish the afternoon, we visited the big daddy of them all, the spectacular new flagship winery of Bodega Catena Zapata, built to resemble a Mayan pyramid. The Catena family has made wine here for more than one hundred years and operates what is probably Argentina's best-known winery, producing some of this country's most highly acclaimed wines.

This day that started at dawn in Las Lenas finally ended with an outstanding, multicourse, multibottle dinner at 1884, the Francis Mallman restaurant in

Mendoza. Mallman is Argentina's hottest young chef, and spending a couple of hours over our multicourse meal here showed us why. Since dinner in Argentina doesn't start until about 11:00 p.m., it was well into the wee hours when my body was finally deposited at Gabriela Furlotti's Finca Adalgisa for my last night. A small private estate and winery, the Finca accommodates small numbers of guests, both in cottages and in the traditional family home which has been refurbished for guests. Surrounded by their private vineyards, this place is an indescribable island of privacy and character, right in the middle of Mendoza. I was already fed up with being prematurely pushed from fabulous places by The Schedule, but only being allowed a few hours here really was the last straw. I contemplated making a stand. I would lock myself in and just refuse to leave. But early the next morning when my ride to the airport arrived, I just didn't have the juice. The Schedule won in a clean sweep, and my reluctant, groggy, and now completely defeated self was being escorted to an airport again, completely against my will.

So that's how I ended up back in Buenos Aires zipping along in a cab, sleep-deprived, and in a state of sensory overload. I had just dashed across Argentina from east to west, into northern Patagonia, and back again, bouncing from shooting fields to lodges, wineries, and ski resorts, to truck-wading and trout fishing, and a little rodeo in the Andes. It had been an attempt to compress time, trying to cram at least three or four weeks

worth of fun into just five frantic days. But now that the haze has finally lifted, a few things have become apparent. There's a whole lot more to Argentina beyond the famous waters. And, while I constantly chafed against my protracted schedule, I probably would have done so even given three or four times as long. Call me a fun-hog, but the fact is, for most fly fishers and wing shooters, there could never be enough time here. Add wine to your recreational vices and you're really in trouble. You see, it's all just a matter of time. So the next time I go to Argentina, the one thing I'll be taking is more time, lots more time.

Rainbow trout, Rio Tordillo, Provincia Mendoza, Argentina

Opposite page:
Rainbow trout, Rio Tordillo, Provincia Mendoza, Argentina

85

CHAPTER 6

The Mouse Trout of Middle Earth
Brown Trout: South Island, New Zealand

Until very recently, all I really knew about New Zealand were basically these four things, in roughly the following order: It produced the world's best rugby players (the All Blacks) and the world's best match-racing sailors (remember the America's Cup?); it boasted a highly touted trout fishery; and it was blessed with a landscape so fantastically incredible that Hollywood cast it as Middle Earth for the hit movie *Lord of the Rings*. From a tiny island nation of just slightly more dirt than Texas with a population of just four million people and some forty million sheep or so, this seemed an impressive, if somewhat peculiarly distinctive list of traits. Besides these few things, though, New Zealand really didn't come into my consciousness all too often.

THE MOUSE HATCH

All this considered, I suppose it shouldn't have come as too big a surprise that as far as New Zealand and fly fishing were concerned, the peculiar distinctions weren't about to end. Most curiously perhaps, I was to learn that although New Zealand may or may not have something like a Mother's Day caddish hatch or any other such bug event you would expect to produce such a renowned trout fishery, what it does have is a mouse hatch. That's right: apparently in New Zealand, mice aren't born, they hatch, or at least they do on the South Island. And not only do these mice hatch, but unlike more conventional and seasonal bug hatches, the hatches are unpredictable, occurring every few years or so, give or take. In fact, a mouse hatch isn't governed by anything you might expect, like air and water temperatures, but rather, by the reproductive habits of the beech tree. Now to put all this in a beechnut shell, as far as I understand the phenomenon, every four to six years the native beech forests of New Zealand experience an uncommonly

88

heavy seeding, or "mast" year, a population explosion of beechnuts that in turn fuels a population boom in mice, and presto—a mouse hatch.

Now to cut to the quick, as far as fly anglers are concerned, these hatches are of huge significance, as this proliferation of rodents means the already famous New Zealand browns get even bigger, merely because of the amount of red meat on their table. In mast years, as the story goes, these already huge and picky trout just lose themselves, gorge on mice, and can grow into what seasoned Kiwi guide John Gemmel refers to as "double-digit fish"—those that exceed ten pounds. And furthermore, there can be a lot of them. But to add further intrigue to this already fascinating situation, the mouse hatch in any given beech forest is pretty much unpredictable: not just its timing, but also, its size and specific location. In other words, you never know where or when a mouse hatch may occur, or how big it will be. But rest assured, if there is one going on of any size it's an event worth knowing about.

Finally, if trying to plan a fishing vacation around a completely unpredictable mouse hatch halfway around the world isn't akin to pounding sand down a rat hole in the first place, the final rub is, even when there is a hatch of any significance going on in any particular river drainage, good luck finding out about it. "Fish and tell and go to hell" seems a common credo among Kiwi guides in the best of times, so when intel comes from down under regarding something as significant as a mouse hatch, you'd best just drop everything and get down there. Yes, truth in life and fly fishing is stranger than fiction, and what I've outlined thus far pretty much describes the peculiar set of real-life circumstances that drew us down under to this peculiarly distinctive country. A mouse hatch in Middle Earth— what serious trouter could resist all that?

Now before I go any further, I have to come clean and commit what most fly anglers would surely see as a blasphemy of sorts. You see, truth be known, as far as trout fishing goes, well, it really doesn't float my boat. Yeah, they're pretty and scrappy, and I've spent countless days of nonstop fun fishing for them, but over the past several years, unless the trout were of the sea-run variety (i.e., steelhead or sea trout), I'd generally become somewhat jaded to fishing for them. Most of the time, or so it seemed, trout were just too easy and just too small. So mouse hatch or not, flying halfway around the world to fish for resident trout—even to a mecca like New Zealand—was neither a blip on my radar screen nor an item on my angling to-do list I was losing any sleep over.

Trout Boy Tim, on the other hand, my colleague and photographer for this report, was as excited about all this as a six-year-old on Christmas Eve. He'd actually bugged out to New Zealand a couple of years back along with his trout buddy, Malcolm the Fly Tier, took up residence in a minivan, lived primarily off Tim Tams (Australian chocolate-covered biscuits) and high-caffeine energy drinks, and literally lived just to fish for

trout. Hard core. I'd never met Tim before this assignment, but this much about him I knew. Lucky thing for me, though, as having a true trout bum like Tim along would surely help me to understand and truly appreciate just what all the fuss was about with regard to the New Zealand trout scene.

But even without his help, and even before the plane landed on Kiwi soil, I got my first inkling that New Zealand takes all this trout fishing stuff rather seriously, as part of the customs and immigrations procedure requires visiting anglers to declare their waders and wading boots for inspection and possible disinfection or fumigation to prevent the inadvertent contamination of streams by unwanted forms of aquatic life, such as didymo (*Didymosphenia geminata*, or "rock snot") introduced from foreign lands. As many places as I've fished, I'd never traveled to a country that listed wader inspection as a condition of entry, and as commonsensical as this sounded, once I'd learned that failure to do so can result in a fine of up to $100,000 or five years in jail, even I reasoned out that there had to be something very special they were protecting.

At 370,000 people, give or take, Christchurch is the largest town on the South Island and the jumping off point for almost anyone visiting this magical land, whether for trout fishing, bungee jumping, whale watching, or any one of several other peculiarly Kiwi thrill-seeker activities. On the more conservative side, *Lord of the Rings* tours to this country have become

Opposite page:
South Island, New Zealand
Tim Romano

89

increasingly popular as well. Indeed, Middle Earth has been growing substantially as a premier tourist destination once it became known that the country is safe and stable, its food and wine superb, the scenery spectacular, and the people really, really nice. And, to make this package even more appealing, in New Zealand they speak English, or a version thereof anyway.

RIVERVIEW LODGE: KIWI TROUTING 101

Our third angling compadre, Mike, had already been in country for a few weeks vacationing with his family, and on news of the mouse hatch, decided to stay a while longer and join us on this peculiar fishing adventure. So we collected Mike at the Christchurch Airport, and the three of us headed off for Hanmer Springs and Riverview Lodge, epicenter of the alleged mouse hatch. Operated by the husband and wife team of John and Robin Gemmel, the lodge is located some eighty miles north of Christchurch on a hill above the confluence of the Waiau, Hanmer, and Percival rivers. The lodge is also the rather luxurious home of Robin and John, fully furnished with large and beautifully detailed guest rooms, a billiard room, bar, fireplace, dining and living areas with huge picture windows, fabulous gardens, a massive party deck boasting unmatched river and mountain views, and an Austrian trained chef and assistant. In addition to all this, for non-anglers, the town of Hanmer Springs offers everything from bungee

jumping to thermal hot springs, and is one of the South Island's most popular alpine tourist destinations. For anglers, the main draws are the nearby rivers where some of South Island's biggest browns are caught each year, as well as the guiding services of John Gemmel and his crew. John is a Kiwi classic with over twenty years of guiding experience in both hunting and fishing in this region. Quiet and soft-spoken, with a dry yet cutting sense of humor, John exudes a professorial air, and it doesn't take long to realize that his knowledge of fly-fishing for trout is comprehensive.

Sitting in the comfort of Riverview campus our first afternoon, Professor Gemmel commenced the course on Kiwi Trouting by building enthusiasm for the subject among his students, namely Tim, Mike, and I. Although by far the youngest, Tim was the smug class suck-up—the irritating kid in the front row who knows all the material down to the ground already and is really just there to show off. Mike was the enthusiastic and goal-oriented one, not quite as experienced a trouter as Tim, especially in New Zealand, but he was eager to learn and even more eager to get a photo of himself for the office wall holding a bigger brown than the one Joe Daniel, editor of *Wild On The Fly*, had of himself on *his* office wall. Boys will be boys, but at least Mike had a goal. I myself still had no real agenda other than to produce this story and a video of this angling odyssey, so not entirely unlike the feeling I had through most of my college years, I felt a bit like I was just taking up

Angler and guide, South
Island, New Zealand
Tim Romano

91

classroom space, you know, for the credits, so to speak. That said, John eased us all into this class rather skill-fully. His photo albums were stuffed with photographs of huge brown trout in the hands of happy anglers, and he proudly pointed out all the double-digit fish. Hmm, maybe I could get with this down under trouting gig

after all. But from that point on, it became increasingly obvious that anything I thought I'd known about trout fishing before meeting John was largely irrelevant, and the fact that I had no idea of what trout fishing, New Zealand–style, entailed became immediately apparent.

Point one: New Zealand browns, mouse trout or

South Island, New Zealand
Tim Romano

92

not, are extraordinarily spooky, wily critters, and everything else revolves around this essential point. So, lesson one in fishing Kiwi-style was that we were to stay well behind the guide at all times as he walked upstream to locate one of these elusive animals, stopping when he stopped and following again at a goodly distance only if and when he chose to continue. When the guide found a fish, he would stop dead and we were to do likewise, approaching him only when signaled to do so, and even then with the utmost caution, staying well out of the water until instructed otherwise. Only when the guide was satisfied that we could indeed see the intended target would he put one of us in position to cast, and our job at that stage was basically just not to screw things up. John warned that even getting in the water could at times spook these trout, as he figured that depending on the currents, they could actually smell you when you got in and even that could put them down. Whew! I'd never heard that one before, and while I wasn't quite ready to question twenty-plus years of Kiwi trouting expertise, since the good professor certainly wasn't above pulling your leg once in a while, to this day, I'm not really sure if he was serious about this one or not.

Staying well behind them and then remaining undetected by these crafty trout was key, so false casts were to be kept to a minimum and made well away from the trout, and when the cast was measured, only the final delivery was to be put directly over the fish. Line 'em, and you were finished. Drag on the fly? Game over. Even brightly colored fly lines or the glint off overly shiny fly rods might put them down. But if you somehow managed a perfect presentation without spooking the fish, you might have a chance—provided you had the right fly on at the time, of course. Otherwise, you'd have to repeat this performance of piscatorial stealth and perfection who knows how many times more, probably with many different patterns, until you eventually screwed up a cast, otherwise spooked the fish, or the fish actually ate.

If you did manage somehow to hook one of these fish, the name of the game was still to try and remain downstream of it. Because of the extremely fine tippets required, even on the big trout, the lesson on fighting and landing was to try to keep the fish swimming upstream to tire itself out, as if it got too far downstream of you, it would be impossible to pull it back upstream on the light tippet. Now most of this seemed like good common sense, if a bit over the top, and despite my relative apathy for the subject, I really was becoming quite intrigued with it all. I was even getting a bit excited by the idea of getting onto one of these hyper-wary trout, maybe even catching and landing it, and I really thought I was generally getting the message. Near the end of the lesson, though, I asked the professor if these trout were ever fished downstream on swung flies (which I thought was a perfectly reasonable question), and immediately knew I'd tripped up. Again reminiscent of my college days, the only reply I got back from the professor was a look that asked, "After everything I've just said, could you really be that slow?"

Professor Gemmel was a little guarded about the specifics of the water we were to fish as we left Riverview Lodge our first day. In fact, up until this point, his replies to all my questions about what river or rivers we were to fish were met with evasive responses, as in, "Ask me no questions and I'll tell you no lies." Seems all the water in New Zealand is open to all guides, and everyone else for that matter, so if you knew where good trout were lying, and you knew that they also hadn't been fished for in a while, it was a pretty good strategy to keep your yap shut about them. Fair enough. I didn't so much care about the exact names of the

93

Opposite page:
South Island, New Zealand
Tim Romano

streams, but my curiosity had been piqued, and I was somewhat eager to get a firsthand look at one of these super spooky trout again, just to see what all the fuss was about.

ON THE WATER

So this day, after a short drive from the lodge, we arrived at a spectacular stream, clear enough for us to easily count the rocks on the bottom, winding through a broad valley surrounded by beech forests. Much of the stream could be seen from the high bank John had just walked us out onto. Just upstream, two braids of the river came together into a narrows and broke in a slight right-hand bend around a gravel bar on the opposite bank. The fast water at the head then spread into a beautiful run studded with big boulders. A clear seam separated the main current, which pushed against our high bank, from a truly sweet glide of soft water on the far side. Although the clouds were low and it was raining lightly, the scenery and river were breathtaking, living up to all the hype about New Zealand. And to complete the picture, holding its position high up in the head of the pool, just off the seam in the soft-water eddy, lay a huge New Zealand brown, a double-digit fish that John knew or strongly suspected would be there. Seeing that hog lying there was truly an impressive sight, even if it was just a trout. And not that I'd had any doubts, but just the sheer size of this first fish, even

looking at it from forty feet up on the bank, went a long way to convincing me of the veracity of this whole mouse hatch thing, as it was difficult to believe that any resident trout could grow to that size in this small river on a diet of bugs alone.

Now for some mysterious reason, we didn't cast to this fish this day. Surely the professor had his reasons. There was some discussion about not being able to get down the bank without spooking the trout, or that it wasn't apparently feeding or looking in the mood to feed, that the weather wasn't right, or somehow, the stars just weren't lining up well enough for us to have a go at this big fish. As I've said, I never professed to be a great student of anything, but regardless of the details, I suspected somehow that the wise professor figured it was just too good a trout to waste on any of us just yet. Again, that was just a guess on my part, but even if I was right, you could hardly blame him for this, for as far as he was concerned, all three of us were just rookies—even Tim was an unknown commodity at this stage. It made perfect sense to assess the level of his students before throwing out the really hard questions. Whatever the case, I did get my first look at one of these big, mythically difficult trout, and as we continued on upstream to find another, I also got my first look at what Kiwi trouting's really all about.

First off, stalking trout New Zealand–style felt strangely closer to upland bird hunting than any sort of fishing I'd ever done before (an impression that was not

diminished by the fact that John had his duck dog with him, a black Lab). Imagine your guide using his eyes rather than his nose to find fish rather than birds. You follow along dutifully, as you would behind a bird dog, since you are not nearly as fit to do the job at hand as he is, and you both understand this fact implicitly. So the guide ranges ahead, searching, ever farther upstream as you saunter along happily behind without a care in the world until the guide suddenly goes on point—and trust me, this really happens. He spots a fish, freezes in his tracks, and you would swear if he had a tail it would be pointed straight up in the air and quivering. You are now on high alert. And then a few moments later comes the wave: The guide motions carefully for you to come forward (granted, as no dog could ever do), you approach with caution, and once alongside him, he points out the fish, which you may or may not even see at first. If necessary, though, he patiently and painstakingly steers you to it, rock by rock, until the fish comes into your view. Then, with a bit of last minute instruction, he allows you to cast. This is your shot. Unlike the explosive flush of a bird and the rapid, reflexive swing of a shotgun, though, at this stage in Kiwi trouting you have time—more than enough to think of everything you've been told about the difficulty of these fish, not to mention the infinite variety of other thoughts that might just creep into your mind at a time like this, things that might just make you, well, nervous enough to screw the whole thing up.

This day, Mike was first up, and outwardly, his unbridled enthusiasm to fish masked any nervousness that he may have been feeling. John spotted a good fish that we could all see lying in the eddy behind a huge boulder that essentially split the main current in half. Although the fish wasn't quite as big as the first one, it was still every respectable ounce of at least five pounds, and sitting less than thirty feet away and in clear view, it didn't seem to be a particularly tall order to catch it. So, under the watchful eye of the professor, Mike stepped in, took his shot, and the fish, like the scenery, lived up to all the hype and was gone before we knew it. Strike one. Tim and I barely had a chance to get our cameras set up before the scene was over. Now granted, Mike's performance might not have been all it could have been, but this was, after all, just his first attempt on the insanely difficult New Zealand browns. Maybe nerves did come into play after all, but whatever the case, the fish was gone and we were about to get our second lesson in Kiwi trouting. That is, when you blow a shot, you could be waiting and walking a long while before you get another.

Indeed, we spent most of the balance of the day doing exactly that, walking behind John and watching Mike blow shots. Well, okay, it really wasn't quite like that. After all, we were hiking up a small gorgeous steam meandering through a broad, pastoral valley flanked by beech forests that looked almost manicured while waiting for John to go on point. For lack of a better phrase,

Opposite page:
Brown trout, South Island, New Zealand
Tim Romano

97

it was a truly enjoyable way to fish. When I asked him once what kept him from getting tired of doing this after so many years, John responded, "Well, you never catch a trout in an ugly place," and so far, I could certainly see his point. As far as Mike's fishing went, well that's another story altogether. His casting did improve, but nonetheless, we were still fishless after the next three or four shots he had this day. And, although this was just our first outing, Tim and I were getting a little concerned that if something didn't change fast we might never get the photos and footage we needed, that is, of someone catching a fish. Mike was clearly getting a little frustrated too. He was, after all, doing as well as most of us would do on our first attempts. Some errant casts were made for sure, but other times, the fish just didn't like what he had to offer. These trout really were kind of tough, and the pressure mounted with each missed fish and each little hike in between. So on the next fish John found, we put Trout Boy up to bat, and lo and behold, the class suck-up produced. Making a relatively long cast up into the head of a pool and across the main current seam, Tim showed us how it was supposed to be done, hooking and landing a very respectable five-pound brown, and the only fish that came to hand this day.

Over the next four days, the education continued as we followed John or his fellow guide, Jonathan Greensmith, through many stretches of many nearby un-named rivers—not that they really lacked names, of course, but one thing I'd learned so far was to stop asking. Except for one day when overnight rains had clouded the waters, each of the streams we fished was gin clear, although some seemed to carry a slight bluish-green glacial tint. Small- to medium-size classic freestone streams, they could all be waded easily and most could be crossed pretty much at will, with no heroics required. Of course, the main bonus to the water clarity was the ability to see fish, and like some twisted little band of piscine voyeurs, we spent hours spying on huge trout sipping off the top as well as "grubbin' on nymphs," as Tim would say. It could be equally amazing just how a six-, seven- or even ten-pound brown trout could remain hidden in the clearest, skinniest water. In fact, on occasion, John or Jonathan would go on point for no apparent reason while we strained both their patience and our eyes in an attempt to see just what we were supposed to be casting to. The point being, even in these crystal-clear waters, stalking trout is a job best left to professionals.

Indeed, everything about trouting in New Zealand was just as advertised in all the brochures: sight-casting to big, spooky trout in gorgeous, beautifully clear streams flowing though spectacular alpine scenery. The only thing that was conspicuously missing throughout our five days, though, were the mice. After all, we'd come clear around the world for this "hatch," so I'd kind of expected to see rafts of them floating downstream like a bunch of big, furry, spent spinners, with huge brown trout inhaling them off the surface. The trout were certainly here, and some real hogs to boot, but so far, there was nary a rodent to be seen. So where were all the mice? And, how could one know whether one was fishing to a "mouse trout" or not?

The professor explained that the actual hatch had taken place some time ago, and that was why the average size of the trout we were fishing to was larger than normal. Even on a steady diet of mice, the fish need a bit of time to bulk up, and since we neither caught nor even cast to a trout smaller than about five pounds, this explanation seemed reasonable. When the trout were actively gorging on mice, John said their stomachs often felt hard and lumpy and could also be visibly distended. But although the main mouse hatch had come and gone, he added that there was still one distinguishing characteristic besides size that indicated that a trout had been most likely feeding heavily on mice: One part of its anatomy could remain visibly inflamed from passing so many of these toothy, bony little creatures. I'd never heard that one before, but it seemed plausible enough, and some of the big trout we examined did indeed look to be in some state of discomfort in that area. However, as mentioned, the professor does possess a pretty dry sense of humor, so there was some room here to believe that he might have just made this one up, taking some sport for himself in watching us closely examine the back ends of all the trout we caught.

GRADUATION

As far as our progress in Kiwi Trouting 101 went, we came to understand early on that Mike's main weaknesses were perhaps somewhat more related to, let's say, time on the water in general, rather than on any kind of performance anxiety. But under the tutelage of John and Jonathan, he made great strides, greatly improving both his casting and his casting-to-catching ratio over the course of the week. Upon hooking up, Mike also got the top marks for style on the "river-rock run," the downstream dash often required to keep up with a fish that decides to head for the sea. Running with his rod held high and screaming "Mama, oh mama!," Mike's runs were inimitable. Furthermore, he actually overachieved in his goal of getting a photo of himself holding a bigger brown than the one on Joe's wall, as he managed to get several shots of fish in the six-pound and over class—far more than enough material to rub Joe's nose in.

Tim, of course, was only there to hone his already considerable skills, and perhaps owing to his performance on day one, the very next day, the professor allowed him to cast to that big fish we saw from the high bank on the very first day. The trout wasn't visible this time, though, as the river had risen and colored up from the previous night's rain, but John suspected that it would be there nonetheless. He directed Tim's cast perfectly, and again, Trout Boy came through, catching not only the biggest trout of our trip, but the biggest

trout he'd ever caught in his life—a brown estimated at just over ten pounds on a tiny Copper John. Overall, Tim did become our go-to guy on the trip, showing us all again and again how living streamside in a minivan for a couple of months can vastly improve your trout angling skills.

As for me, I did get manage to add a couple of wily New Zealand browns to the list of fish I've caught, and the angling was indeed some of the most peculiarly interesting trout fishing I'd ever done. As a long-standing trout school dropout, I definitely needed work on skills like straightening out fifteen- to eighteen-foot leaders and making perfect presentations with just ten feet of fly line out of the tip top. There was also little doubt that I got a failing grade from John on my fish-striking abilities. Somehow, even when I managed to entice a trout to take my fly, wet or dry, most often I was so mesmerized by the spectacle that I'd wake up only after the fish had long since spit it out, at which point the professor would ask a rhetorical question like, "Were you planning to strike that fish today?"

Despite all this, I have to admit that New Zealand and the professor did put trout fishing into a whole new light for me, capping it all off in the last hours of our last day when John walked us out to a hefty eight- to nine-pound fish he'd marked earlier in the day. We all sneaked up to it and watched it feed happily for a few minutes from a high grassy bank directly above. From my casting position downstream, I could no longer see the fish, but with Jonathan beside me, Mike behind me with a video camera, and John and Tim directing my casts from the high bank, we spent no less than forty-five minutes on this fish, emptying Jonathan's entire fly box on it in the process.

Drift after drift, for what had to be at least a dozen fly changes, the fish continued to eat everything floating down past him except what I was throwing, and with each cast and each refusal came scintillating color commentary and all manner of advice from the professor and the rest of the peanut gallery. "He didn't even look at it. Try again . . . It looked like he twitched a fin that time . . . Why don't you try casting it closer to him? . . . Hey, you just about lined him that time . . . Woops, he moved up a few feet . . . You might have spooked him . . . No, wait, he's still grubbin' . . . Okay, he had a good look at that one. Change the fly." On and on it went, and everyone, including me, was on the edge of his seat, no doubt wondering if the fish would take before I screwed up a cast. The suspense was unbearable.

Finally, in a last-ditch effort, we decided to show this trout a big furry mouse. And while there was every chance that just the sheer size of the fly alone might spook him, we were in mouse-hatch country, after all, and at this point, there was little left to do. So I tied on a mouse pattern, and as it happened, this was the only fly so far that this fish even really acknowledged. Excited chatter erupted from the spectators almost as soon as this comparatively massive piece of fluff landed. After almost an hour of trying, the fish

moved decisively toward the fly shortly after touchdown, had a good look . . . and flared off it at just the last second. We were instantly re-energized, and no doubt owing to all this additional excitement, my next cast was abysmally ugly. In fact, I might as well have just thrown a rock at him, as I crashed the huge, half-drowned mouse fly pretty much right down on the fish's head and then, just to make sure the screw-up was complete, let it drag through the pool at warp speed. Needless to say, the fish was frightened into oblivion, and I was booed and hissed from the folks up on the grassy knoll.

Still standing knee-deep in the stream with my fly line now trailing below me, I was certainly disappointed, but there was now little question in my mind as to just what all the fuss was about in regard to Kiwi trouting. These trout were anything but too small, and neither were they anything close to being too easy. In fact, the whole deal, including the hiking upstream to stalk them and running back downstream to land them, was really a lot of fun. So much fun, in fact, that if John ever calls again with news of a mouse hatch, I might not be able to resist. I may even be compelled to drop everything, fly halfway around the world, buy a trashed-out old minivan, and spend a little time streamside on the South Island. On second thought, a far better plan would probably be to sign up for Kiwi Trouting 201 and stay on campus again with John and Robin at Riverview.

Opposite page: South Island, New Zealand

101

CHAPTER 7

Viva Cuba Libre!
Bonefish, Tarpon, Permit: Cuba

Jean Marc really wasn't quite sure just what he'd done on the second day of his first saltwater fishing trip ever. Sitting in the comforts of the air-conditioned lounge of the Casa Batida Fishing Club in Cayo Largo, Cuba, he somewhat innocently asked, "Eez eet true zat zee pearmeet eez zee most deefficult feesh?" The rest of us didn't quite know what to say, but collectively, our response amounted to something like, "Yeah Jean Marc, some people try for years before getting a permit." We were all waffling between delight for his wonderful achievement and all-out green-eyed envy after listening to his tale of landing a sixteen-pound permit earlier that day. That's right, a permit—a sixteen-pounder. Remember, Jean Marc had never fished a tropical saltwater flat before in his entire life; Cuba was his very first kick at the cat.

This fact notwithstanding, the charismatic French cardiologist and passionate steelheader really didn't seem to believe all the hype or our collective reaction. "I am sinking zat zee tarpoon eez zee most deefficult, as zey don't take my flies," was his sincere, if somewhat skewed outlook on the whole flats fishing scene. Gimme a break. This guy just didn't seem to get it. It was kind of like trying to tell a guy who got a hole-in-one in his first round that golf was indeed, hard. In retrospect, though, as the intensity of my seething jealousy has somewhat abated, I can sort of see his point. After all, even as an avid and well-traveled angler who was obviously well aware of the difficult reputation of this species, Jean Marc had hooked and landed one of the first, if not *the very first* permit he ever saw! To him, taking permit on the fly was as easy as falling off a log. You could understand how he might be confused by a room full of people telling him otherwise. Nonetheless, had his own amazed delight or easy natural humility been anything less than what they were, someone in

Opposite page:
Havana, Cuba

that room, maybe even me, would have surely dragged him outside and at the very least (in a purely celebratory fashion, of course) thrown him off the dock *Mais l'attente, mes amis,* this gets even better.

The following day, my fishing partner Hans and I were leisurely being poled along one of the vast, white, unpopulated flats of Cayo Largo, searching for bones and marveling at just how perfect life can look sometimes, especially from the bow of a flats boat. It was early June off the south coast of Cuba. It was probably just over ninety degrees, but we had enough wind to keep the temperature manageable and the casting just this side of unmanageable. The skies and sea were clear, and our whole world was a tropical angler's dreamscape awash with watercolor shades of azure and white, at once smooth and rippled and intermittently interrupted by the opposing greens of turtle grass and mangrove, all of which was periodically and most satisfyingly shattered by shards of quick-swimming silver. We had indeed already been into several bonefish this day, including one of about seven pounds, and a doubleheader our guide Marco orchestrated by getting us to leave the boat, wade onto a mudding school, and execute a one, two, three, cast routine. Everything was perfect, and made even more so by the fact we saw no other boats whatsoever. Even envy was a positive contribution to this day, as Jean Marc's first permit had raised our hopes and anticipation to a slightly higher plane than that of a regular fishing day. In addition to having

tropical paradise all to ourselves, we thought maybe, just maybe, Cuban permit might prove to be really stupid too. Certainly, the bones we'd encountered so far weren't nearly as freakishly paranoid as their Keys cousins. We were hopeful.

DOUBLE GRAND SLAM

Just then, though, a confusing little bit of bedlam broke loose in our hopeful little corner of paradise. A staccato stream of excited Spanish suddenly exploded from the radio, and Marco scrambled madly off the poling platform to respond. Hans and I were suitably perplexed by the goings-on until one phrase we understood came crackling through loud and clear in the three English words "double grand slam!" We went from confused to incredulous in three short words. While Marco was getting the details of the event in Spanish, Hans and I mulled over a concept neither of us probably ever anticipated having to grapple with in the course of our angling lives, that is, what constitutes a double grand slam, anyway? Is it both anglers in the boat, each with a grand slam, or one guy getting both himself? Of course, both would qualify, we decided, but the chances of either one actually happening seemed about as likely as a one-legged man winning an ass-kicking contest. Impossible. Surely, we had misinterpreted the message. Never mind the Bay of Pigs, this one sounded more like a tale from the Bay of Flying Pigs. In the peculiar excitement of the

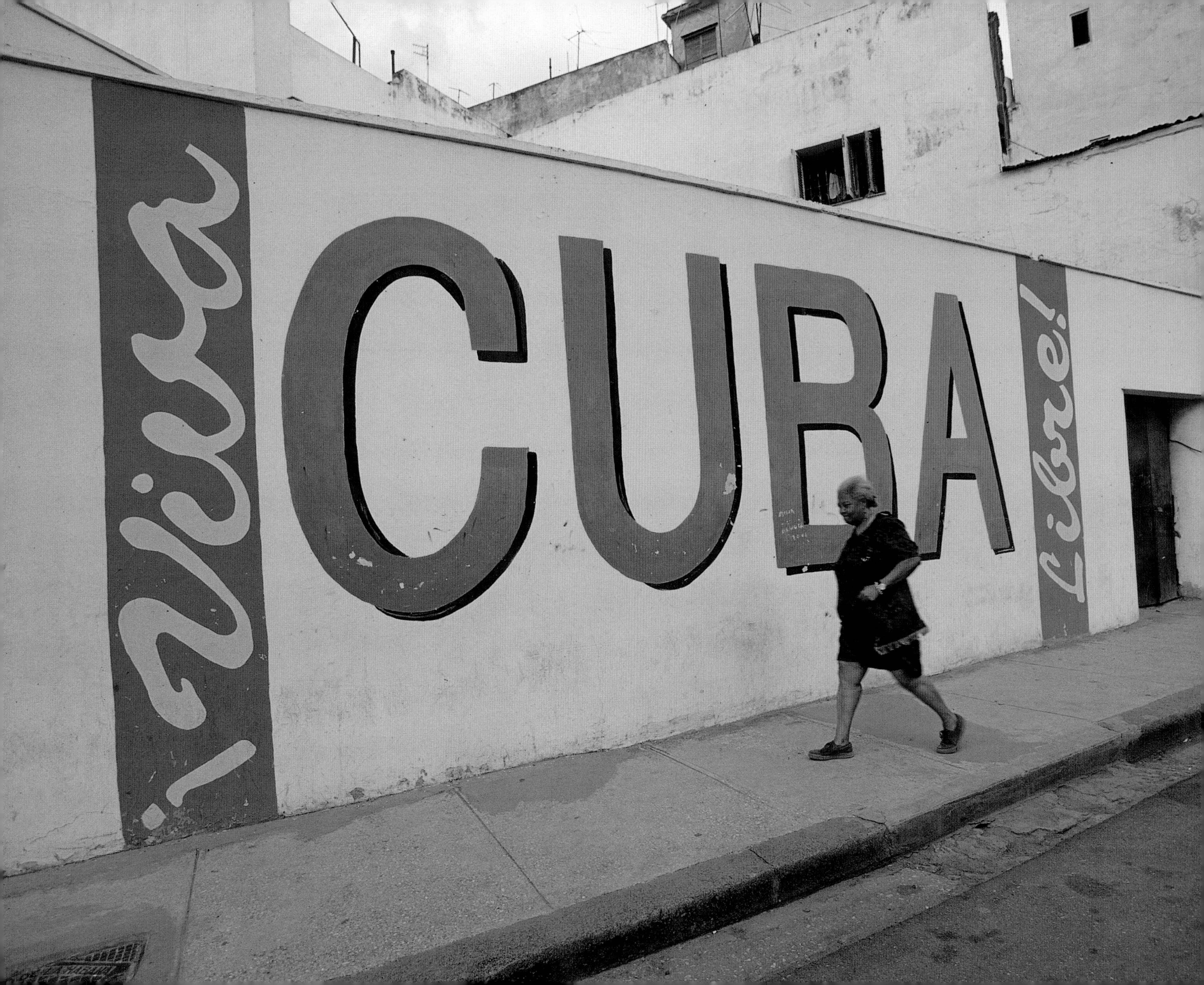
¡Viva
CUBA
Libre!

Opposite page:
Jardines de la Reina, Cuba

moment, however, we had neglected to factor in one highly significant detail. We had forgotten that Jean Marc Frey was on this trip too.

That's right, my friends, believe it or not, Jean Marc had indeed pulled off the near impossible. Fishing alone, on the third day of his first flats fishing trip ever, the French fishing fanatic had not only doubled his previous day's permit count, but also added two tarpon, and at least two bones just for emphasis. It was as if he set out to prove without doubt that permit number one had been no fluke. If his performance the previous day was the equivalent of a new golfer getting a hole-in-one, this day, Jean Marc had gone out and broken par. In case this is happening too fast, allow me to recap. Three days of saltwater fly fishing in Jean Marc's entire life thus far amounted to three permit, two tarpon, and at least two bonefish landed. *Sacre bleu*. Pardon my French, but could this guy really be this good right out of the gate? Was he the Tiger Woods of saltwater flats fishing? His results did seem to indicate that something other than just dumb luck was at play here, and besides, could a guy even be *that* lucky? Outside these considerations of luck, skill, and the possibility of genuine angling genius, could it in fact be the case that the Cuban flats were really this good? Over the next ten days or so we would get the chance to try and answer this question by getting a firsthand look at the fishery here, which, thanks to Jean Marc, already had some fairly grand expectations to live up to. One thing about Cuban waters, however, was already fixed in my mind: Later today, Jean Marc was going to swim in them.

Double grand slams and angling genius aside, there is no conceivable reason that the flats fishing in Cuba should be anything less than outstanding. After all, Cuba has some pretty fancy neighbors, being surrounded by some of the world's best known and highly visited flats fishing destinations: the Florida Keys, Bahamas, Caymans, Turks and Caicos, Belize, and Mexico. Geographically, it is certainly in the right latitude and time zone, and its waters lay claim to more than four hundred keys and smaller islets with thousands of square miles of associated flats. Furthermore, in addition to these attributes of great geography and habitat, politics has kept Cuban angling resources both underdeveloped and underutilized. By any form of reckoning, Cuba is a veritable preserve, and a big one at that, smack dab in the middle of angling paradise.

Our two-week glimpse into some of what has been developed here for fly fishing took us to two separate operations, both joint Cuban/Italian ventures located off Cuba's southern coast. Our first week was spent fishing from the Casa Batida Fishing Club in Cayo Largo del Sur, the site of Jean Marc's double grand slam. Our second week was aboard the Tortuga, a floating lodge situated in the Jardines de la Reina (Gardens of the Queen), a long string of islands and keys also off Cuba's south coast but farther to the southeast. Havana was mission control. So, in between fishing sites, we were forced to spend a few nights under the spell of this storied and intriguing old city. It would be a rough stint all right, but for the sake of journalism, we were willing to endure the hardships.

HAVANA

Havana. Home of Ricky Ricardo, birthplace of the daiquiri, and, of course, capital of Fidel's fiefdom. To the locals, *la Habana*, to almost everyone else, Sin City of the Caribbean. Just saying the word conjures up steamy, sultry, sinfully passionate and romantic images, all shrouded in the thick, sweet smoke of fine Cuban tobacco and bathed in the smooth seduction of minty, rum-filled *mojitos*. Visions of pirates, gamblers, and gangsters dance in your head alongside those of movie stars, rebels, and revolution, topped off by fantasies of flirtatious overtures from luscious, exotic, dark-eyed *chicas*. That's the short version of the standard hype about this town, and even in its current state, Havana delivers. Okay, maybe there aren't any pirates and gangsters left, and granted, the trappings aren't nearly as swank and shiny as they once were, but somehow the ambience persists. Indeed, from the moment you get out of the airport, it seems you've stepped into a time warp to a place that's still a lot closer to the bad old days when Papa himself used to drag his talented, gin-soaked carcass down to *el Floridita* to get potted on daiquiris.

Since those times and the revolution, the Cuban economy has been in the tank, and especially so since the fall of the Soviet regime, which was the last great economic influence propping up this Caribbean communist experiment. Of course the greatest single effect on Cuba, that of the powerful and over forty-year-old American embargo designed to destabilize Castro, has instead kept this country in a sort of suspended animation, which is now overlaid with a palpable poverty manifested in a distinct lack of goods. Even before we left the airport this became immediately apparent as a fellow traveler was having his bags inspected. They were jammed to the zippers not with clothing and personal effects, but with lipstick, nail polish, soap, shampoo, and all manner of other inexpensive day-to-day items, making it look a lot more like he'd just been nabbed for looting a dollar store than merely trying to enter a country. Outside the airport, this curiously confusing picture was completed by the scores of cool, classic 1950s-vintage American cars that cruised by in living color in a scene that would have seemed more at home in a black and white movie. Some of these retro rides did look their age, but others gleamed like they had just rolled off a line in Detroit. Even if you weren't a car nut, you couldn't help but be impressed by this Caribbean concourse of classic American metal. If you were a car nut, your trip was already made.

Opposite page:
Bonefish, Cayo Largo, Cuba

CASA BATIDA FISHING CLUB, CAYO LARGO

Leaving Havana for our first destination of Cayo Largo was a little like going from the sublime to the ridiculous. It was like being plucked from the pages of *Islands in the Stream* and being placed on the set of *Fantasy Island*. Gone was all the considerable history, intrigue, romance, and distinction of one of the oldest cities in the Americas, and in its place was a manufactured tourist playground that could have been almost any beach resort anywhere in Mexico or the Caribbean. We left a time warp of decaying colonial architecture, classic American cars, and an economically struggling society set against an ironic background of propaganda billboards extolling the virtues of socialism and the revolution. We arrived in a culture of hedonism and relative affluence, an isolated outpost of motor scooters, cookie-cutter condos, uniformed staff, pool bars, and sunburned vacationing foreigners, mostly European and French Canadian. Not that there's anything wrong with all that, but it's certainly a switch from the Cuba you see in Havana.

Casa Batida anglers use any number of the resort accommodations on the island, and are shuttled to and from the fishing club each day by air-conditioned bus. This week most of us found accommodation at the Sol Club, a modern all-inclusive complex that houses several restaurants, bars, and even a large outdoor theater that hosts exercise classes in the afternoons and fairly

extravagant song and dance performances most eve-nings. The overwhelming majority of guests here are non-anglers. (When was the last time you attended an afternoon aerobics class at a fishing lodge?) Indeed Cayo Largo is a perfect place for those anglers whose paths of least resistance lead directly to angling destinations of this variety. Here, right next to world-class fishing are spectacular beaches, sailboat charters, great snorkeling and scuba diving, exercise classes, tennis, horseback rid-ing, even a small turtle ranch, as well as a nearby colony of tame iguanas. A win-win situation, if you will, for the traveling angler/non-angler duo. The only compro-mise here, for the hard-core angler would seem to be the lack of the total fishing-lodge experience—the total, twenty-four-seven, single-minded focus on angling and angling-related bull sessions that for some are essential to a true angling vacation.

Cayo Largo is actually the second largest island in the Archipelago de los Canarreos, located about 110 miles southeast of the Cuban capital. Around it lie a cluster of small islands and keys, 140 square miles of which is designated as a restricted Natural Reserve by the Cuban Government. The Casa Batida Fishing Club has exclusive rights to fish in this preserve, which is closed to all commercial fishing, except for lobster.

As promised, we were met at the airport by Mauro Ginvera, Manager of Casa Batida, and taken directly to the clubhouse, where we were first introduced to Marco, "the best guide in Cuba," according to his boss.

110

We were immediately inclined to agree, as even before the introductions were over, he inspected our reels and lines, surveyed our flies, strung our rods, retied our lead-ers, and had a couple of Crazy Charlies looped on and ready to go before we'd even changed into our fishing clothes. We were out of the air-conditioned clubhouse and onto exclusive water within minutes.

All of the associated flats, channels, and lagoons within the preserve, as well as those outside it, are sec-tioned and rotated among the Casa Batida guides. In our week there were just five boats, eight anglers total, working this vast area. On our first day out, we hap-pened to meet up with two anglers on a lunch stop at a secluded beach, but that was it. For the balance of the week, every flat, channel, or lagoon we fished seemed as if it had been created for our sole pleasure. Most of the flats here are wide with white-sand bottoms, but there are occasional fields of turtle grass. Many areas are shal-low enough to wade, and because of their soft sandy bottoms, can be waded in bare feet.

We found bonefish scattered liberally across all of these sandy flats: singles, doubles, schools, big schools, mudders, tailers, you name it, and on the white sand they were usually quite easy to spot. Most were in the two- to five-pound class, with occasional fish to seven or eight pounds. Permit were also plentiful and fairly often found traveling within big schools of bones. Although we didn't encounter any tailers, we had countless shots at traveling permit. Unfortunately, none that we encountered was quite as stupid as Jean Marc's early results had led us to hope. On two occasions, bonefish at the last moment took flies cast at permit, and one absolute knee-weakening permit tipped on my fly but either didn't eat it or was missed because of operator error. Over the course of the week, we got tired of catching bones and overdosed on adrenaline from the number of permit encounters. Unfortunately, we only saw a few tarpon and got no shots at them but happily filled out our cards with abundant catches of jack, mutton snapper, and barracuda.

Each morning upon arrival at Casa Batida, we were met by our guides and very welcome shots of great espresso waiting for us in the clubhouse. Each afternoon, our fishing day ended here in an equally welcome air-conditioned environment that now featured cold beers and Cuba libres. Mauro, who has a restaurant background that shows, always laid out a small snack of terrific pasta, soup, or other delicious creation to help fortify us after a hard day of fishing. In addition to this level of pampering, our *après*-fishing brag sessions in the clubhouse provided a valuable outlet and an opportunity to purge ourselves of a measure of the angling bull that would be lost or underappreciated by the large and painfully pink majority of exercisers back at the resort. To the appreciative, however, the information passed on in these sessions did serve one important function: It provided a far more accurate picture of this fishery than any that could be fairly gleaned from

only a week of fishing. And perhaps not too surprising, the rather profound picture that emerged was all about grand slams.

To put this picture of slams in perspective, consider the fact that in 2003, IGFA registered just thirty-four inshore grand slams (permit/bonefish/tarpon) worldwide. Of course, not all of them are registered but it is still a telling yardstick. Grand slams just don't happen all that often. Double grand slams, of course, are even rarer. Besides Jean Marc's marvelous achievement, only one other double was registered with IGFA in 2003. Another detail about Jean Marc's tour de force that is equally incredible is that his lifetime permit-to-cast ratio at this point was a staggering three to five, and that alone has to be some kind of a record. (Somehow, his first two casts didn't produce any permit. Go figure . . .) In 2003 Casa Batida anglers recorded thirteen grand slams. Our week was twenty-three in the club's season, and these were the overall stats for eight rods during that time: bonefish, 243 landed; tarpon, 19 jumped and 7 landed; permit, 3 landed; jacks, snapper, barracuda, sharks—lots landed. And finally, to add anecdote to arithmetic, it was obvious that had we focused solely on bones and not dallied on other frivolous distractions like permit, tarpon, jacks, and the like, the number of bones caught this week could easily have been doubled.

Getting back to grand slams, we also learned that of the eight anglers at Casa Batida this week, five had scored Cuban grand slams. In addition to Jean Marc's

two, fellow angler Gareth Jones of Airflo Lines got a grand slam here on May 8, 2002. (The very next day his fishing partner, Tim Hughes, got one too, but for the purposes of this piece, we don't even have to count that one). Also, on March 13, 2003, Jack Simpson of Simpson's Angling in England and his fishing partner Richard "Dick" Hatfield, also from England, got double grand slams—one each, from the same boat on the same day, fishing out of Tortuga lodge in the Jardines de la Reina. So, just how good are the flats in Cuba? Well, this week and in this crowd, they were good enough to make you feel almost like you'd been skunked if you hadn't slammed. So how good is that?

There is an old angling axiom that states you should never leave fish to find fish, but that's what our schedule forced us to do, as our astounding, eye-opening week at Casa Batida came to an end. The good thing was we were scheduled to be at the Tortuga in two days. So while we were unquestionably breaking the rule, we had the unique consolation that we were indeed leaving the site of one double grand slam and going to another. Getting there though, was another matter altogether.

TORTUGA LODGE,
JARDINES DE LA REINA

The westernmost end of the Jardines de la Reina archipelago is only about 140 miles to the east and slightly south of Cayo Largo. Since there were no direct flights between these two sites, however, we were forced to make a long, circuitous journey some four times that distance. First, we backtracked northwest to Havana for the night. To our great pleasure and good fortune, double slammers Jack and Dick were in Havana this night too. Not only are they highly accomplished anglers, they are also wonderful company and frequent travelers to Cuba, and we derived tremendous benefit from their intimate knowledge of the ins and outs of Cuban travel and angling. "When you get to Jardines, send our regards to Pepe and try and fish with Koky as your guide—he's highly excitable but a great guide," we were told. This was one of the best of many tips we got. They also pointed out that while Koky spoke very good English, his accent made "cast" sound like "cat," so not to be confused. Finally, having made the trip many times themselves, they warned us that we faced a long and tedious travel day. Hans and I thus were able to take steps this night to ensure some of tomorrow's tedium would be tempered with a hangover.

Very early the next morning, we reluctantly left Havana and flew west along Cuba's northern shore to Cayo Coco, which itself is a part of a huge chain of keys and small islands stretching off Cuba's northern coast. Here we began a three-hour bus ride that retraces the historic Moron-to-Jucaro trail, which runs almost directly north-south through the central province of Ciego de Avila and ends up on the southern

Opposite page:
Jardines de la Reina, Cuba

113

Opposite page:
Barracuda, Cayo Largo, Cuba

mainland coast in the tiny fishing village of Jucaro. This route, which passes through largely agricultural land, was once a fortified barrier of trenches, wire fences, and hundreds of listening posts built by the Spanish to repel the western push of Cuban forces led by Maximo Gomez in the 1895 War of Independence. While the line was eventually breached, some of the fortifications still stand; they are considered national historic monuments and are visible from the road. From Jucaro, it is a five-hour boat ride to the Tortuga Lodge, which is situated some sixty miles offshore in the Jardines de la Reina and operated by Avalon's Fishing and Diving Center.

For our five-hour boat ride over blue water, we were accompanied by several Cuban lodge staff who didn't speak much English, and by Chris and Greet, a charming Belgian couple who luckily did. These two had actually accompanied us all the way from Havana, having booked the week at Tortuga for the diving. For the course of our long blue ride, we filled our time by trying to explain things like double hauls and double grand slams to our new non-fishing friends, and in turn, they educated us about the wonders of the diving world. Out at the Jardines, the draw for divers is the world's third largest barrier reef, which runs along the 150-mile archipelago, and the abundant sea life it supports. For Chris and Greet, diving with sharks was also one of the anticipated highlights. Strangely, in what would seem to be the height of the fishing season, Hans and I were the only anglers making this voyage.

Avalon's is the only operator in this archipelago, which is almost as long as the entire Florida Keys, and we were their only two anglers this week. If it seemed like we'd had it all to ourselves at Cayo Largo, here in the Jardines de la Reina, we truly did.

The Tortuga is a floating hotel, a large, two-level barge outfitted with air-conditioned staterooms for the guests on the top deck, with kitchen and dining facilities on the main. Fully loaded, she accommodates up to twenty-four anglers in bunked staterooms, each with its own full bathroom and shower. While relatively small, the staterooms are air-conditioned, very clean, and more than adequate. Since we had the run of the joint this week, Hans and I each took a separate room, so we had the additional luxury of being able to spread our stuff all over the place. In direct contrast to the surroundings at the Sol Club, the Tortuga is all fishing lodge. It is a true home for the hard core, tucked away in a secluded bay in the middle of an otherwise uninhabited archipelago the size of the Florida Keys, boasting a relaxed open-air bar on the back deck within spitting distance of the moored flats skiffs. Even the staterooms here are named after the various species of local fishes, and the dining room walls are covered with photographs of fish, happy anglers with fish, and, not surprising, a bunch of grand slam certificates from IGFA. The closest thing to an exercise class here is climbing upstairs to the top deck at bedtime following a strenuous evening of bull sessions at the bar on the back deck.

Permit, Jardines de la Reina, Cuba

116

could flip easily and quickly between love and loathing. Whenever you made good honest casts or caught fish, Koky loved you, and the exchange was straightforward and typically went something like this:

Koky: "Sir! Tarpon comeen, eleben o'clock, sitty feet, moobeen righ, moobeen righ . . . "

Angler: "Okay, I see it."

Koky: "Cat now! Cat now! More righ! More righ! Stop the fly! Perfect cat! Streep eet. Steep! Streep! Stirike!"

Angler: "Yahoo! He's on!"

Koky: "Let een go. Good Cat. Beautiful!"

Conversely, when you made bad casts, or weren't paying attention, or choked, Koky instantly switched to loathing, and the latter part of the exchange was decidedly less congenial, more like this:

Angler: "Huh? What? Where?"

Koky: "Eleben O'clock! Cat now!"

Angler: "Okay, but I don't know where . . ."

Koky: "More righ, I say more righ! Stop the fly, stop the fly! No! Cat again, cat again! Long cat! More righ! Ah, sir! Bad cat, berry bad cat. Look at me, *look* at me [pointing]. Thees eez righ, thees is lef. I say more *righ*! Ah! Tarpon moobeen berry fas."

On one particularly bad stretch of "berry bad cats," Koky couldn't help himself any longer and actually jumped off the platform, relieved me of my rod, and gave me a quick but intense casting lesson. While this was a little abrupt, it was worth it to see him cast, as he

Victor Jose Morales Gonzales, aka "Koky," indeed turned out to be a key component of our Tortuga experience. And he was everything Jack and Dick told us and more. He is a consummate flats guide, and no doubt because of his mostly European clientele, one of his first questions to us was, "Do you want distances in feet or meters?" Koky is a small, wiry man, quick as a flea, intense as an osprey, dogged as a bloodhound, and, as described, highly excitable. We quickly learned that when it came to fishing, he was also as fickle as a spoiled housecat. Depending on the situation, Koky easily double-hauled quick, tight loops ninety feet into the wind in perfect casts both forehanded and backhanded. While that's something you normally don't want to see after you've blown a series of casts, Koky's clinic was instructive and did confirm that my equipment, at least, was capable of doing the job. Joking aside, this was all just part of a very genuine guide/angler teamwork that, sadly, isn't always there but definitely develops when fishing with Koky. Within the first few hours, it became abundantly clear that he wanted fish at least as badly as you did. Within the first day, it was also equally clear that Koky would enthusiastically pole you to the end of the earth, then perfectly position you for a good shot at a fish, but in turn, if you blew that good shot by putting any less effort than that into your cast, he'd kill you—simple as that. When a guide works as hard and well as Koky, I think that's more than a fair deal, and the most enjoyable and fruitful way to fish the flats.

That's Koky in a nutshell, and thus, not only did we have the flats all to ourselves, we couldn't have had a better introduction to the unbelievable fishing at Jardines de la Reina. Having arrived here well and truly sated on bones from Cayo Largo, we told Koky right off the bat that the only things that mattered this week were permit and tarpon. We felt like the ultimate spoiled flats brats, and he was more than happy to oblige. Arrival day only left us a few hours in the afternoon for fishing, but a quick run to close-by Caballones yielded a tarpon

of about fifty pounds. This was a very promising start to our week and our initial look at the flat we would eventually end up calling "Koky's Office."

Our daily drill for the week was to start here on tarpon, and then, depending on the tides and how well the tarpon were fishing, go looking for permit. Unlike the fishing areas at Cayo Largo, which are all in relatively close proximity to one another and mostly sandy, the character of the keys and flats in the Jardines are set on a much larger and more varied scale, ranging from sandy turtle grass flats to deeper, hard-bottomed ones populated with coral. In fact, the Jardines are not at all

Tarpon, Jardines de la Reina, Cuba

117

unlike the Florida Keys, except that they are uninhabited and there are no other anglers.

From Caballones, which is just a few minutes from the Tortuga, we sometimes ran over deep, open water for close to an hour to reach a new flat. Once there, however, Koky would find permit within twenty minutes of arrival on a surprisingly consistent basis. If he didn't, we'd just pick up and move to another flat. If the tides or the permit weren't cooperative, we'd often end up back at Koky's office on tarpon. Admittedly, on a few brief occasions during the week, we did relent and spent a bit of time on bones, which on one day in particular turned out to be absolutely unavoidable.

On this day, day four to be exact, we set out as normal and started the day by jumping three tarpon. Unfortunately, none was landed. By this time, in addition to our spoiled contempt for bones, we were also growing accustomed to a fairly high standard of tarpon fishing. In fact, on a previous day, from the time we started fishing at about 8:30 a.m. to when we quit at about 2:30 p.m., we spent no interval longer than twenty minutes without some kind of action on the silver kings—situations where we either had a decent shot at one, jumped one, or hooked and landed one. The action was so consistent that I actually timed the intervals in between. To be absolutely candid, this observation came as a by-product of more selfish motivations, as I initially started looking at my watch just so I could

haul Hans off the platform when his turn was up. Unattractive behavior maybe, but being the spectator seems interminable when the fishing's hot. The upshot of all this is that when Koky suggested early on that we leave to go search for permit, we didn't give it a second thought. We could get tarpon anytime . . . or so we thought at the time.

Permit so far had been quite a different story, so we arrived at the Cuervo/Cucaracha flats considerably less cocky. Within a few moments, though, we were rewarded with the simply sublime sight of big permit tails waving in the air. Hans and I each had one good shot at a tailer

Cuban guide, Jardines de la Reina, Cuba

Opposite page:
Tarpon, Jardines de la Reina, Cuba

in fairly short order, but sadly, neither ate. Then, shortly after 10 a.m., we were onto more tails. Hans was up, made a perfect cast, the permit ate, and our world was turned on its ear. If we'd thought Koky was excitable up until now, he might as well have been dead compared to how he reacted to this. As the permit made its first blistering dash and before Hans had even cleared the line or let out a triumphant whoop, Koky came out of his skin and remained there for the duration of the fight. Chaos and jubilation swept across our small skiff and were immediately joined by tension and high anxiety. At least 150 yards of backing instantly melted off the reel, and almost as quickly, the sea fans and corals, heretofore largely unnoticed, magically seemed to grow and multiply into an impenetrable, leader-shearing forest through which the permit fled at warp ten. Koky poled like crazy and screamed like crazy while Hans gamely attempted to comply with the sometimes impossible instructions he was getting in the battle to subdue his first permit ever. Happily, though, the fish stayed stuck, found deeper water, and after what seemed like both an instant and several forevers, the fight was eventually won. This time, Koky jumped off the platform to land the fish and then instantly grabbed Hans in a bear hug. With permit in hand, he was golden. It was barely 11:00 a.m. when the dust settled. Photos and high fives were finished, a well-exercised permit was released, and we found ourselves firmly on the exciting but uncertain road to a possible grand slam.

In fact, the only certainty at this point was that I wouldn't be fishing again for the balance of the day. Great. Not only was I afflicted with a serious case of permit envy for the second time in Cuba, this time, I had to be envious from the confines of the spectator seat. So, while I pretended to be a gracious, well-adjusted angler, we sped back to Koky's office with the intent of holding a successful meeting with a tarpon. Hans's interaction with the tarpon, though, proved to be long, tense, mostly frustrating and sometimes exasperating struggles. The meetings were, however, filled with many episodes of high excitement, as over the next few hours, Hans jumped no less than six tarpon, all of which fit somewhere in the forty- to eighty-pound range.

We had indeed been into fish like this on all the previous days, but with a permit on the scorecard and a slam in the offing, the stakes were definitely raised and tarpon fishing had taken on a whole new dimension of added urgency. For a while it seemed everything that could go wrong, did. Fish came unbuttoned, casts were blown, lines didn't clear, fish broke off, and on one particularly painful occasion, Hans got a loop of line around his wrist that, had the class tippet not broken, may have given that tarpon a true "hands down" victory. Even from the stands, post-permit fishing was a highly exciting activity, unfolding as it did this day as a cross between classic screw-up and outright slugfest. The good thing was, the tarpon kept coming and Hans kept going. And, after a few hours of truly hard work,

120

a well-earned sixty-pounder finally allowed itself to be held and photographed with an exhausted but ecstatic angler, and we were two-thirds of the way home.

It was just after 3:00 p.m. when all that stood between Hans and his grand slam was one measly little bonefish, and thus the bonefish of Jardines de la Reina rose in our estimation from shunned to desperately sought after. But now that we finally wanted to dance, the question was, would the wallflowers be willing? In Hans's favor, Cuba's bonefish had so far proved a fairly accommodating lot, so our hopes for completing the slam were high. True to form, Koky did his part and located a large school fairly quickly, and on this day, all the stars lined up for Hans. After just a couple of shots, the grand slam was made in an almost anti-climactic fashion. Indeed, after tangling with a twenty-five-pound permit and slugging it out with a six-pack of silver kings, in the end it was the little three-pound bone that looked as if it might just tip Hans over as he raised it above his head in exhausted triumph. It was truly a remarkable achievement in one of the most memorable fishing days I've ever been witness to. I was sincerely happy for him, and not just because it meant I could fish the next day . . . although the thought did cross my mind.

That evening, we most appropriately celebrated Hans's Cuban grand slam on the back deck of the Tortuga with what else but shots of twelve-year-old Havana Club on ice, a steady stream of Cuba libres to follow up, and a box of Monte Cristos. Of the group of eight anglers we were a part of over this two-week period in Cuba, this day Hans had put himself in the very distinguished and unlikely majority—those who had slammed. Anywhere else, and in most any other random group of anglers, it's a safe bet that the grand slammers among them will be a tiny minority. Beyond the testament to all of these anglers' considerable skills (and those of their guides—Koky himself has guided twenty-eight grand slams), this statistic is also a profound testament to the quality of fishing in Cuba.

Ten grand slams were recorded in Tortuga in 2003. Interestingly, ten permit were also recorded, and as it turned out, everyone who caught a permit also got a grand slam. This stands in slight contrast to the numbers at Casa Batida, which for 2003, show twenty-two permit caught over all and thirteen grand slams. Together, the twenty-three grand slams attributed to these two fishing operations alone in 2003 account for two-thirds of the total number of grand slams registered with IGFA that year. Again, while not all slams get registered, that is still a thought-provoking stat and incredible fodder for future angling bull sessions.

BACK IN HAVANA

Before we knew it, we were sitting in the rooftop bar of the Hotel Ambos Mundoz in the center of old Havana, sipping on Kristal beer and listening to a live trio of

121

Cuban musicians playing "Guantanamera." We had just come upstairs from touring Ernest Hemingway's old room at this hotel, which is preserved as nothing less than a shrine. Earlier this day, we'd completed leg one of our Papa pilgrimage by visiting the Floridita and downing a couple of obligatory (and expensive) daiquiris in his honor. Tomorrow, time permitting, we planned to complete the Hemingway Slam by visiting Cojimar, the small fishing village that was the backdrop for *The Old Man and the Sea* and longtime home to Gregorio Fuentes, the author's old friend, pilot of the *Pilar*, and the man who many believe was the inspiration for Santiago himself. After an amazing two weeks of fishing, how cool was it now to be spending time atop a real bit of Cuban-American sporting and literary history and unwinding by hanging out in some of Ernie's old haunts?

Indeed, Cuba seems to have it all: a long and fascinating history and culture, a venerable sporting heritage, the world's best rum and cigars, and for flats anglers, a serious shot at a grand slam. Cuba also seems poised on the brink of sweeping political change in regard to its long-standing stalemate with the United States. One thing is certain: Fidel is approaching his eighties, and even he can't live forever. When things do tip here, the quality and quantity of angling opportunities that could become available are simply mind-boggling. While much of Cuba's sport fishing resources have been sheltered as a by-product of politics, it seems that the Cubans have also recognized their tourism value and have protected them in reserves and national parks, as is the case with both locations we visited. If you're not an American and live to fish the flats, go to Cuba now. If you are an American, and are willing to be an outlaw angler, I would offer the same advice. If you are a law-abiding American angler, don't despair. As long as the conservation ethic remains, I can only think that Cuba will get even better as time passes and the fishing resources there are developed to their full and considerable potential.

Finally, since this story is really all about slams, I'll leave you with one more. From post-trip e-mail correspondence, I've just learned that Jack Simpson slammed yet again at Tortuga on November 19, 2003, nearly eight months to the day since his last one there. Good work, Jack! That makes seven grand slams attributable to a group of eight otherwise ordinary anglers who happened to fish together in Cuba in the Spring of 2003. Maybe the current American policy toward Cuba has one thing right: Fishing this good really ought to be illegal.

Opposite page:
Cayo Largo, Cuba

123

CHAPTER 8

Sea-Run Char by Chopper

Arctic Char, Lake Trout, Grayling: Nunavut, Canada

ichael was casting into the head of a pool about 150 yards upstream when it happened. My two other guests, Joe and Ken, were fishing the lower pool beside me. It was an idyllic Arctic afternoon of blue skies and gentle breezes, and we were working an unnamed stream flowing through the rolling Canadian tundra. Situated at about 68.10° north and 106° west, we were well above the Arctic Circle, and just west of the middle of nowhere.

I was looking upstream, watching Michael fish in a very productive pool with every expectation of seeing a bent rod at any moment, when abruptly, in the kind of awkward urgency most often seen in folks who suddenly need to vomit, he abandoned his cast, spun 180 degrees, grabbed his day-pack, and inexplicably began an arms-flailing, bat-out-of-hell flight, as if he was being swarmed by bees. A person running in waders is always entertaining, but with a fly rod in one hand, a pack

in the other, and obvious panic in his heart, Michael's wader-sprint was particularly stylish. He also threw in a couple of world-class face plants into the boggy tundra along the way, adding considerably to the drama of this already curious event. Then, over the sound of the rushing water came a shrill and panicked explanation: "Bear! Bear!"

Damn. Arctic barren-ground grizzlies are common here, so I pumped a slug into the chamber of my Remington 870 insurance policy and started my way up toward him, expecting hungry brown rage and fury to come hurtling over the rise at any moment. A multitude of thoughts raced through my mind. First, a quick assessment of the situation and calculation of the odds. Over one hundred yards between me and potential bear. Short slug barrel. My deadly aim. Sorry, Mike, but at that moment, my money was on the bear. Then again, I could've sworn I'd said "don't run from the

A-Star helicopter, Nunavut, Canada

Opposite page:
Wilberforce Falls, Nunavut, Canada

see who got to deal with the bear rather than having to meet some of the other day-to-day challenges this operation required.

Not that any of it was as bad as a bear mauling, but setting up and operating a frontier sport angling operation using helicopters in the middle of the Canadian Arctic has its share of, well, peculiar challenges. The Arctic territory of Nunavut alone (which before 2000 was part of the Northwest Territories), comprises about two million square kilometers, roughly the size of Alaska and California put together. The human population is about thirty thousand, and no road connects it to the rest of North America. With no roads and virtually no people, it is a vast expanse of seemingly endless tundra, dotted and crossed by countless lakes and streams and encompassed by a rugged coast of bays and islands that few will ever see and even fewer will ever fish.

Out here, even a seemingly simple task like keeping yourself in fuel involves a major production. It also doesn't help too much that the helicopter goes through the stuff at a rate of 180 liters per hour. So for us, moving guests around means first moving drums of Jet B, cold-weather jet fuel, across the frozen sea ice of the Northwest Passage. This happens around March or April with temperatures at thirty below zero, while the ice is still good and thick. Like a scene out of Road Warrior meets The Ice Man, a Cat train (huge sleds hauled behind a D9 Caterpillar tractor) heads across the frozen Arctic loaded with fuel to position our main

bears" during our safety talk back at the lodge.

This scene was unfolding at tail end of Arctic Heli-Fishing Adventures's second season of operation, and we'd already been through some pretty interesting situations just to be able to bring groups of anglers out here. So while I was taking Michael's situation anything but lightly, I knew that given the choice, my business partner Martin and I would have fought each other to

Arctic Poppies,
Nunavut, Canada

Opposite page:
Parry Bay, Nunavut, Canada

Prior to getting ourselves into all this, Martin and I had held various roles in the fly-in sport-fishing lodges of British Columbia. Between us, we had covered everything from guide/boat boy to owner and had worked together on many projects, so we were well initiated in dealing with anglers and remote places. As the world turned, Martin ended up in Yellowknife, Northwest Territories, running a helicopter company, and our paths crossed again as I was traveling through "The Knife" en route to a film shoot in the high Arctic. Having made a few trips to the far north over the last ten years or so, I had heard many incredible accounts of Arctic sport fishing, and in his time in Yellowknife, Martin had collected his share as well. Considering our past association, fishing was the natural topic of conversation:

"Hey I heard about these guys chartering a twin and going into this beach on Sommerset to cast flies to huge schools of big Arctic char, sea-runs, hanging off the beach waiting to go upstream . . . Well, Alex was telling me about his family going out around Kazan Falls in the Spring. Thick with char, thirty-pound lakers and lots of grayling . . . Apparently it's unbelievable at so-and-so, and have you heard of this-and-that, and . . . " On and on it went. Charts were consulted, beer was consumed, and a classic evening of fishing stories ensued.

To say there is no lack of spectacular sport-fishing opportunity in the Arctic is a colossal understatement. It is the land of trophies. The IGFA world records in many categories for lake trout, Arctic char, and grayling

cache. About the same time, some one hundred nautical miles to the southwest, a secondary cache is positioned by Skidoo and *komatiq* (Inuit sled). Our Inuit partner Peter (more on him later) performs this feat alone, in frigid conditions, one or two drums at a time, and the trip can take more than an hour each way. Sound outrageous? You should see our fuel bill, and that's just the beginning.

Sea run Arctic char, Nunavut, Canada

Opposite page: Arctic grayling, Nunavut, Canada

between across an enormous expanse of the Canadian Arctic. Dirty job but it had to be done. At first, it was pure adrenaline, with our faces pressed to the windows and asking the burning question, "See any fish down there?" Invariably, "Holy shit! Look at 'em all!" was the response, and like kids at Christmas, we would land, run out into the water, and start casting even before the blades stopped spinning. After a while, though, the question became, "See any big ones?" If the answer was, "Nope, don't see anything huge," we'd just kept going. How quickly we humans are spoiled. When you can leave a school of two hundred sea-run Arctic char in a virgin stream or lake and just keep going because you didn't see anything "big" from 150 feet aloft, you are to be pitied as a truly jaded angler. But that's what happens when you add helicopters to the Arctic angling landscape.

So, the angling dream was indeed there, but countless Arctic dreams have been turned into waking nightmares by logistics, and our rude awakening was now upon us. Besides its sheer size, Arctic Canada is devoid of infrastructure as we know it in "the south." Things as common as airports with scheduled jet service, hotels and lodging, even food and fuel cannot always easily be found, at least not in the way we needed for the kind of angling experience we wanted to provide. Helicopters were one part of the solution, but a lot more needed to fall into place even before they became practical.

are from the waters of the Canadian Arctic. And, these records are especially telling when you consider that an overwhelming percentage of the water up here never even gets fished at all. The problem is not the lack of terrific fishing; the problem is getting to it. We just had to check this out.

So for the next two seasons we applied helicopters and creativity to this huge land of almost unimaginable angling promise. We fished a multitude of virgin water systems, from beach to lake and everything in

Sea-run Arctic char,
Nunavut, Canada

132

communities that enjoy scheduled jet service with a good connection to the south, and the lodge, while remote, is in shooting distance.

Our plan was to partner with local business by bringing our services in the form of helicopters and our experience in the sport-fishing industry, but we hadn't quite figured on how and where. After all our looking, a half-hour phone conversation with Luke produced the answer. We would use their facility during their off seasons, which luckily were our peak seasons, and add our fishing operation. Along with a helicopter, that meant providing more amenities and all the services we knew that anglers require. To these ends, we brought our own gourmet chef from Vancouver and provided a well-stocked open bar, a humidor full of Cubans, and a big box of flies.

An unexpected bonus of our partnership with Elu Inlet Lodge has been the cultural component brought by Martina, Mary, and Peter. They were born on this land, and their ancestors left the stone tent rings, fox traps, and caribou blinds behind in archaeological sites that we see often during our travels across what is their traditional home. Some of these sites date back as far as ten thousand years, and, not surprising, many of them appear at locations we just "discovered" to be our best fishing spots. At Elu Inlet Lodge, we are treated to tales of Inuit life, learn Inuit games, witness throat-singing and drum-dancing performances, all of which contribute immeasurably in the making of a true Arctic angling adventure.

ELU INLET LODGE

Along those lines, serendipity intervened in the form of Peter and Martina Kapolak, an Inuit couple from the outpost hamlet of Umingmaktok (population sixteen), and their in-laws, Luke and Mary Coady of Cambridge Bay, Nunavut. (Martina and Mary are sisters.) This enterprising foursome had recently built Elu Inlet Lodge, a tourist facility south of the hamlet of Cambridge Bay with a view to running eco-tours. Cambridge Bay is one of the few Arctic

Our first trip to see the lodge coincided with our first real look at the Spring fishery, and both came as quite a shock. The lodge was indeed more than we could have asked for. Brand new, insulated, heated wooden buildings with full electric power, showers, and laundry facilities in this remote location are far above Arctic standards. Having looked around fairly extensively, we found the lodge worlds beyond anything we had expected. Elu Inlet Lodge was a shock, but a pleasant one.

As for the Spring fishery, char migrate seaward from lakes in the Spring, and the best fishing comes as soon as there is enough open water for the fish to move. Seeing what this actually looks like was the second shock. At the end of June, this region still looks the way most people imagine the Arctic always looks—white and icy. All the moving waters are open, of course, as well as the estuaries and the inflows and outflows of the lakes. But at first blush, this largely frozen world looked pretty grim to us, especially for fly fishing.

THE MYSTERY CHAR OF ITIBIAK LAKE

Itibiak Lake is a char lake about a ten-minute walk from the lodge, and the short stream draining it into the ocean flows through the lodge property. We knew the lake was still icebound, but the stream was running well, so we walked up to the lake to check the status of the outflow. When we got there, we saw that the ice was still so thick it touched the lake bottom. It was impossible to imagine

133

Caribou, Nunavut, Canada

even the skinniest char squeezing out from under all that, so our mood pretty much hit rock bottom too.

It had been a very long day of flying. We were exhausted and now depressed. Ice fishing was definitely not part of the plan. It was near midnight, and Martin and our pilot Cory just retired to the cabin, as there didn't seem to be much else to do. I decided to have one last smoke and take a stroll along the beach. Since we were now in the twenty-four hour daylight period, this midnight looked and felt more like early morning, and the open-water patch of ocean was as flat as a

out of the surface—lots of them. At first I thought they might be tiny rocks being exposed by a receding tide, as they were so close into shore, but as I approached, waves of char streaked away into the open water. They were indeed getting out of the lake—somehow! I rushed back into the cabin, grabbed my fishing gear, and excitedly relayed the information to Sleepy and Grumpy, who either didn't believe me or, at that point, didn't care. For the next hour and a half, I emptied my entire vest sight-fishing to char often in less than two feet of water and sometimes within a rod-length of the shore. However, over that period of time this first night, the elation of knowing the fish were getting out of the lake was slowly and painfully replaced by the frustration of not being able to get them to take a fly—*any* fly. It was so bad I even thought of throwing a spoon.

The Spring fishery subsequently did pan out as planned and is indeed spectacular, as there is more than enough open water to fish and the fish are indeed stacked up in it. We see them from the air, and there are some big ones down there. However, the puzzle of the char in front of the lodge continues to this day. It's now a running joke, as on still nights we can see them from the lodge windows. We set our guests up for it in advance, telling them our trained char should arrive at any minute, and so far, they always have, coming in on the high tide right around midnight. No one has yet caught one on the fly. The kicker is that on spoons, it can be a fish a cast.

Lake trout, Nunavut, Canada

mirror, faithfully reflecting the whiteness of ice and wisps of clouds in a pale blue sky. The ice-floe edge beyond was animated by flocks of eider ducks, and the only sound breaking the eerie Arctic silence was the murmuring of the eiders as they settled in for the night.

But then as I walked and smoked, contemplating our predicament and gazing out at the surreal Arctic environs, I saw them. Tight along the shore were what appeared to be the tiny points of fins and tails sticking

134

Having expectations like this turned on their ears is a constant in this frontier fishery. Since we cover so much territory, learning the habits of the fish and timing all the systems leads to many surprises and discoveries. That's the truly unique and greatest part of what we get to do, and we've got enough territory to last several lifetimes. So far, we've barely scratched the surface, but have already experienced some pretty strange and wonderful things, like sea-run lake trout, for instance. Bet you didn't even know there was such a thing. We have seen an entire stream bottom move as the shadow of the helicopter passed over it. Actually it was the backs of fish, so plentiful and stacked in so tight that before they spooked, we thought we were just looking at a dark rock or sand substrate. We catch Spring char that are obviously mending "kelts" (fish that have recently spawned) and right beside them their fat, nickel-bright brothers, which show no signs of winter wear. We have watched ambitious lake trout of twenty and thirty pounds follow a hooked cousin of equal size or better right to the shore in an obvious attempt to eat it. And reviewing measurements recorded after just our second season, we suspect we released char that would have broken current fly-caught records. Unfortunately, many of our experiences fall into the UFO category—that is, most of the time, no one really believes us. Fortunately we now have witnesses. We also have numerous tried and true hot spots that increase by the season, but we also know the next surprise is never too far off.

River X

One current unsolved mystery is River X. It was so hot we named it after Lake X, where they allegedly perform all those ultra-clandestine outboard motor tests. Just from whom we are keeping our secret we haven't quite decided, since no one but us has fished here in living memory. In the Spring of 2001, we found two pools here that produced double- and triple-headers of lake trout over twenty pounds on cast flies pretty much all day, every day for a week. We caught the occasional char and grayling as well. It was almost stupidly good but pretty typical of what we had come to expect from a hot spot.

In the fall of the same season, we rushed back, only to find our hot spot mind-bogglingly barren, comparatively speaking. We caught the occasional lake trout, but nothing big, and the fishing required a level of work we had long since grown unaccustomed to and certainly never expected here. Strangely, the grayling were present in force, almost as if they had turned the tables and eaten all the huge lakers that were here before. We searched for our missing fish from the air, well above and below our secret pools, but found nothing. For Martin, Geoff (our pilot), and I, it was like we'd had a collective hallucination earlier in the year, and if we hadn't had photographs from the spring, we

might have all ended up on some shrink's couch. Still, we couldn't wait to go back and see what would be going on next spring.

MICHAEL'S BEAR

River X, in fact, is the very place our hero Michael was fleeing from his bear, and I soon had closed enough distance between us to put the odds somewhat back in his favor. Still, there was no bear coming hot on Michael's heels. Michael's partner Joe walked up with me, and with the familiarity of years spent between them, said with a smile, "I bet it was just another one of those caribou." Insensitive maybe, but not completely implausible, as a few caribou had loped by earlier. (Never mind that caribou have antlers and bears don't). When we finally met up, Michael stuck to his story: "Bear, over there, big, brown, and furry." Joe was obviously still skeptical of this and suggested we walk up to the top of the rise and have a look.

I didn't like his idea. Alone with no helicopter and with medical help perhaps days away, going out of our way to look for a barren-ground grizzly was to me a heretical notion. But curiosity and persuasion eventually prevailed, and as we reached the height of land, we glimpsed the rounded back of Michael's big, brown, furry friend as it disappeared behind a small hill just ahead and about forty yards to our right. This was no caribou. It wasn't a bear either, but in Michael's defense, Joe and I understood how the mistake might be made. Then in a scene reminiscent of prehistoric times, it reappeared. A magnificent lone musk ox, with its imposing curved horns and the sun glistening off its long flowing hair, turned and walked majestically toward us and down the very hill where Michael had just set the Arctic record for the sixty-yard wader sprint. The musk ox was indeed big, brown, and furry, and we all just watched with our jaws to the ground, a bit of relief, and a great deal of awe.

At moments like that, you forget about logistics and just marvel at where you are, standing there, fly rod in hand, lost in time in the middle of one of the last true expanses of wilderness left on Earth. Must be a dream, an Arctic dream.

Elu Inlet Lodge,
Nunavut, Canada

137

CHAPTER 9

Daughters of the River Gods
Taimen, Lenok, Grayling: Huvsgul Province, Mongolia

Once upon a time in Mongolia, legend has it that a rather ballsy young shaman named Dayan Derkh ran off with the wife of none other than the mighty Genghis Khan, one of the most fearsome warrior-conquerors the world has ever known. A fairly impressive move in itself, you must admit, but with the mighty Khan in hot pursuit, Derkh was finally cornered in a cave near the Urr River in remote northern Mongolia, and with no other means of escape, he turned himself to stone. Faced with this innovative tactic, the clever Khan countered equally creatively by summoning the aid of the Dalai Lama, who sent seven Tibetan monks to pray at the base of this cave to remedy this curious situation. Eventually, their prayers convinced this powerful, now stony-faced (if somewhat ambitious) shaman to convert to Buddhism, and an important monastery bearing his name was built on this sacred site commemorating the epic event. Whatever became of the footloose Mrs. Khan remains somewhat clouded by historical haze, but in the interests of happy endings, let's just assume she was safely returned to her rightful spouse and that they lived blissfully ever after.

Okay, great, but what does any of that have to do with fishing, you might ask. Well, strangely enough, more than you might think. Fast forward to the fall of 2004 and to the banks of that very same Urr River where just eight hundred years ago (give or take), and not too far from where we stood, the Khan vs. Derkh precursor to Desperate Housewives reached its dramatic conclusion. This day, Deke Welles, and Bill DeHoff, two fly anglers from Ohio, and our guide Dan Vermillion and I had just left our jet boat and indeed found ourselves walking up the bank, fly rods in hand, to the very site of the Dayan Derkh Monastery. We, of course, were not drawn to this same remote corner of the world in search of a wayward wife, but of something perhaps equally

Opposite page:
Eg/Urr River, Huvsgul
Province, Mongolia

mysterious and compelling—the fabled giant taimen of Mongolia.

As the largest salmonids on earth, these ancient landlocked salmon can reach weights of nearly two hundred pounds and lengths up to six feet. In the stretch of river we were fishing, specimens over fifty inches are caught by fly fishers on a weekly basis, and the heaviest recorded catch tipped the scales at over seventy pounds. And get this—they eat dry flies. In fact, besides their great size, the next most famous taimen trait is their legendary savagery, as they are known to attack explosively almost anything that dares to skitter across the surface of the water, which, in addition to dry flies, includes ducks, mice, gophers, and whatever else might have the misfortune or misguided audacity to chug across a river holding a population of these savage fish. (You didn't think they could get that big just eating bugs, did you?) And as if that were not enough, opportunities to sight-cast to these Asian behemoths are also not uncommon in these crystal-clear waters. With sporting characteristics like these, and a home in the pristine river systems hidden deep within the remote and exotic heart of the historic Mongol Empire, the taimen is arguably the Emperor of the Exotics, one of the undisputed holy-grail species for the serious been-there, done-that traveling fly angler.

But getting back to the monastery for a moment, we were there partly because our quest to mess with the Mongolian mauler had so far come up a little short. After a couple of days of serious questing, we had yet

to engage in any kind of real conquering. So midway through this day, Dan suggested we make a visit to the monastery site, partly as an interesting cultural and historical diversion, but also because a nod of respect to the local deities probably couldn't hurt. Unfortunately, all that remains here today are a few charred poles and beams, since the original monastery, like most others throughout the country, was razed in the wake of the communist religious purges of the late 1930s. The site itself, however, remains sacred to the local people, and in recognition of the resurgence in traditional Buddhist beliefs, a movement is currently under way to re-establish this once important monastery.

As we were to learn, it is customary to leave an offering of respect when visiting such sites, and while this one sits in a very remote corner of the country, the few remaining original poles are festooned with banners of colorful blue ribbons and cloth. Also, placed carefully around the site, tucked neatly within the folds of cloth, are everything from bottles of water, to notes of Mongolian currency, to cigarettes and small children's toys, each item carrying with it the hopes and prayers of some past pilgrim.

Our wishes, as frivolous as they were, were directed toward tangling with a trophy taimen, and as fly fishers, we naturally decided our offering should be a fly. And equally naturally, in the course of our deliberations, someone innocently suggested that it might be prudent to leave one that we weren't likely to need in the

Eg/Urr River, Huvsgul
Province, Mongolia

something that means something to you. Buddha's not stupid, you know!" We stood humbled and corrected. And, whether we knew it or not, this was just lesson one in how taimen, Buddha, ancient spiritual beliefs, modern science, fly fishing, and the very future of this species were all inextricably intertwined. But for that afternoon, anyway, we respectfully left our best flies and departed the Dayan Derkh site to continue our search for a giant taimen, knowing only how dangerously close we'd come to really screwing up our karma.

Now, if this isn't already one of the weirdest fishing stories you've ever read, don't give up on me just yet: I'm just getting started. After all, going on a fishing trip to Mongolia is probably the most mind-bending angling vacation any of us will ever take, so exotic, in fact, that truly meaningful cultural comparisons are almost impossible to conjure. That said, here are a few brief attempts. Go to Buenos Aires, and you'll see the tango. But in Ulan Bator, Mongolia, my friends, you will see contortionists. In France, the culturally definitive beverage is, of course, wine. In Mongolia, it's *airag*—fermented mare's milk, as in horse. And finally, even for responsible catch-and-release anglers, this next one is more than a little frightening. In British Columbia, a violation of the freshwater fishing regulations carries, at worst, a $100,000 fine and one year in prison. In Mongolia, taimen are considered to be the daughters of the river gods, and according to an ancient Mongolian religious scripture, killing one will

coming days, and since the nearest fly shop was probably in Tokyo, that idea did seem to carry more than a modicum of common sense. But as we all searched our boxes for a throwaway bug, Dan quickly pointed out the error in our pathetically earthly and pragmatic ways. "Hey, guys, you better not do that," he warned. "This is a sacred site. The offering you leave here has to be

result in the suffering of 999 human souls. Let's face it; Mongolia's not easy to get your mind around. Indeed, most people's general knowledge of this country seems to end at Genghis Khan and the Mongol hordes, and more than half of the people with whom I discussed this trip eventually ended up asking, "Where exactly is Mongolia, anyway?"

Well today, what's left of an empire that once covered most of the Eurasian continent now occupies slightly less space on the globe than Alaska. Geographically,

Taimen, Eg/Urr River,
Huvsgul Province, Mongolia

Taimen, Eg/Urr River, Huvsgul
Province, Mongolia

Opposite page:
Taimen flies, Ef/Urr River,
Huvsgul Province, Mongolia

144

are composed not of buildings, per se, but of *gers*, the traditional Mongolian felt tents. The city center is still dominated by the ubiquitous grand parade square so favored by the Soviets, and it's quite easy to imagine the rows upon rows of tanks and missile launchers that must have once trundled across this square in strict formation not that long ago. Today, though, it seems populated mostly by small clusters of local artisans trying to sell watercolor paintings to tourists. And, while virtually every painting was of *gers*, horses, camels, the Gobi Desert, or Genghis Khan on horseback, they still carried an authentically distinctive flavor long since lost in the more homogenous tourist kitsch you might find closer to home. This is still one capital city where McDonalds and Starbucks have yet to take over every street corner, and where fridge magnets and "I Love Mongolia" T-shirts are yet to be discovered as bait for the local tourist traps. Indeed, since it's scarcely been fifteen years since western tourists even began to visit this country, Mongolians aren't yet experienced enough with the true horror of the Tourist Hordes to warrant setting up the traps in the first place.

Mongolia is buried like a peach pit in the center of Northern Asia between the vast expanses of Mother Russia to the north and massive China to the south, so it's little wonder the country remains well off the radar screen for most of us. And for practical purposes, reaching the Mongolian capital of Ulan Bator from North America means a minimum of twenty-four hours in transit either through Beijing, China, or Seoul, South Korea.

As a longtime satellite capital of Soviet Russia, Ulan Bator is a curious mix of the standard, overbearingly utilitarian Soviet-style architecture surrounded by traditional, nomadic Mongolian anti-architecture, meaning many of the neighborhoods surrounding the city

HANI TOM TUUL OR "WHERE ARE THE BIG TAIMEN?"

Among the initial adventurous trailblazers to Mongolia was fly angler and outfitter Jeff Vermillion of Sweetwater Travel, who mounted an exploratory expedition in 1995

into the northern regions of the country in search of trophy taimen. Traveling with local guide Purebdorj Shirendbin, or Puji (Pooh-gee), Jeff found pristine river systems still with healthy populations of very large taimen, and, incredibly, part of what he learned is that these trophy-size fish could be taken with dry flies. It was without doubt the finest fly fishery for large taimen left on earth. Puji and Jeff became partners, and their companies, Huvsgul Travel and Sweetwater Travel, became the first and only outfitters introducing adventurous fly anglers to Mongolian fly fishing. Now, almost ten years later, this partnership is still going strong, and thanks to a strict catch-and-release policy and a strong emphasis on responsible resource management on the rivers they fish, catching trophy taimen here remains as good as it was when Puji and Jeff originally discovered the fishery.

The clear, wild waters of the Eg-Urr river system in northern Huvsgul province were part of this original discovery and where we spent our week of fishing. From Ulan Bator, it's a further three-hour flight in a Russian MI-8 helicopter to Huvsgul province, which shares a border with Russia and sits due south of massive Lake Baikal. Just minutes after lifting off in the orange MI-8, we saw the open expanses of the Mongolian steppe stretch to the horizon in all directions. These vast semiarid grasslands seem to roll on forever in a flowing, treeless landscape of subtle earth tones, periodically punctuated by the occasional small *ger*

camps that appear only as a few tiny white dots awash in a limitless sea of land. In a country where livestock outnumber people twenty to one, these small encampments always have a small makeshift corral nearby and are generally surrounded by fairly large herds of horses, goats, and cattle. Just a few miles removed from the capital city, most evidence of the twenty-first century disappears, replaced by scenes of a nomadic herding

Ger camp, Eg/Urr River, Huvsgul Province, Mongolia

Opposite page:
Eg/Urr River, Huvsgul Province, Mongolia

lifestyle that probably hasn't changed much in five hundred years. After a short refueling stop in the small town of Bulgan, we continued toward the Russian border and into the northern regions of Huvsgul Province. Here the rolling steppe gives way to more mountainous, forested terrain, and our anticipation grew as we also started to see clear winding streams twisting their way out of these picturesque mountains.

Had we any inkling what was actually going on at the camp as we approached, however, those already heightened levels of anticipation would most certainly have shot straight through the roof. Unbeknownst to us, as the previous group of anglers was awaiting our arrival and their return flight to Ulan Bator, a huge taimen had been caught. As the story goes, after refusing repeated offerings, this trophy-size fish finally ate and was successfully landed just minutes prior to our arrival. We were met, therefore, not by what one normally expects to be a fairly subdued group of anglers resigned to the fact that their fishing vacation is over, but by a group of guys still vibrating from the thrill of one of the biggest and easily the most witnessed catch of their entire trip. Not only did that group of happy anglers leave on a high, but we also started our trip with indisputable evidence that we had indeed landed right in the heart of trophy taimen central. This was real. *Hani tom tuul?* Right here, brother.

Fishing from three separate camps, Sweetwater provides access to some ninety miles of the Eg-Urr river system (the main stem) and an additional forty miles up the Eg. We were based in the middle camp, just upstream from the confluence of the two rivers, and like all three, our camp was essentially a little *ger* village furnished with a main dining lodge and a common shower facility. Each *ger* accommodates two anglers very comfortably in traditional Mongolian style, and while outwardly resembling a massive white mushroom, upon entering one of these circular felt-lined tents and looking up at the colorful spoke-like ceiling struts, you feel as if you've just stepped under a giant cocktail umbrella. A small central wood-burning stove provides heat, and besides a few modern additions like beds and a lightbulb (and ignoring the waders hanging from the rafters), while in the *ger* you can easily imagine yourself as a nomadic herdsman hunkered down in a Gobi sandstorm, or a warlord of the great Khan resting up from yet another hard day of pillaging.

As far as our own plans for conquest were concerned, as I mentioned, Deke, Bill, and I had fished for a few days but so far had yet to stare down the big one. From the time we'd arrived, the last big taimen this camp had seen was the one that was caught just before our arrival. Trophy taimen fishing, much like steelhead and Atlantic salmon fishing, is not a numbers game. Covering water is key, and there's a lot of it here. Luckily, wading and casting is easy, mostly along wide and gentle sand and gravel bars, though boats are sometimes used to fish the stretches with high banks or slough mouths, which would be difficult or impossible to wade. The Urr is a fairly broad and shallow river, especially above the confluence with the Eg (which appears to dump what looks like glacial color into the system), and has probably the clearest flowing water I've ever seen anywhere. In fact, while zipping along in the jet boats, we found this clarity a bit unnerving, as the shallow bottom was so clearly visible and it seemed like we were flying a lot closer to the rocks than we should have been.

Almost counter intuitively, though, this extremely clear water doesn't require small flies and delicate presentations. In fact, "small" and "delicate" are two words that don't apply to any aspect of taimen fishing. The general angling technique employed, while similar to steelheading, is more of a marriage between swinging a skater across the current and popping a top-water bass bug. The idea is to cast across current and chug your fly all the way through the swing in quick, short, splashy bursts, in much the same way as a small mammal or duckling might struggle its way across the surface. Taimen are anything but shy, so this entire presentation is made complete by using a fly about the size and shape of a small drowned rat, often riffle-hitched to keep its little nose riding high out of water (Chernobyl Squirrels and Verminators are the two top patterns). And finally, as guide Charlie Conn drilled into us on our first afternoon, you have to be ready. Taimen strike suddenly and violently, so if you're messing with your line, or gazing at the scenery, or otherwise asleep at the

Eg/Urr River, Huvsgul Province, Mongolia

wheel, in Charlie's words, it's "game over."

Over the course of the week, casting from both the shore and from boats, we covered many miles of good taimen water. We fished water that resembled classic steelhead runs, likely looking slots, troughs, seams, and slough mouths and all the other places where taimen were likely to hang. Although we had yet to connect with a giant, within a day or two we had all indeed been

broken in on taimen in the thirty-inch range, and even the surface violence that these "little" ten-pounders were capable of unleashing was impressive and definitely addictive. While taimen generally come as singles, on one particularly memorable afternoon, guide Carl Evenson put us on a run that produced an episode I'm sure even he didn't expect. After about half an hour of two-stepping down this particular run with Carl fishing behind me, my little drowned-rat fly came under taimen attack just as it straightened out on the dangle. The taimen overshot the fly in its first attempt and tried a second lunge as I continued to pop the fly straight back toward me in what was probably only a foot of water. It missed again, and didn't return, but just as I turned around to relay all the excitement to Carl, his fly was pounded by a second aggressive taimen. We had run into a little taimen feeding frenzy, and for the next twenty yards or so down the run, it seemed like we were getting hit on virtually every cast, hooking up to at least five fish in what seemed like just five minutes of nonstop action.

On a day-to-day basis, this level of activity was normally only provided by lenok, one of the two other game species available here. Also referred to as Manchurian trout, this species belongs to the same subfamily as taimen, Pacific salmon, Atlantic salmon, and char. Lenok look like a hybrid mixture of every trout you've ever seen but with a curious, slightly downturned, almost sucker-like mouths. They are colorful

Taimen, Eg/Urr River, Huvsgul Province, Mongolia

Opposite page:
Eg/Urr River, Huvsgul Province, Mongolia

151

and heavily spotted and appear to carry parr marks into adulthood, giving them a very distinctive appearance. However, perhaps the most appealing lenok trait, considering the time it can take between taimen strikes, is that they are plentiful and more than willing to play.

Opposite page:
Eg/Urr River, Huvsgul
Province, Mongolia

Fishing them as you would any three- to five-pound trout, we found these fish would eat floaters dead-drifted, dragged, or skated, and just about anything else you threw at them and in whatever fashion. Grayling are also present in good numbers here, but all the ones I saw were tiny ten-inchers, and the greatest entertainment they provided for me was watching Ralph and JD one afternoon trying to catch one in a race to complete the Mongolian grand slam: taimen, lenok, and grayling on the same day.

A TALE OF THE TROPHIES

We were now more than halfway through our week, and despite our best efforts and intentions, Deke, Bill, and I had yet to produce the trophy taimen. I was starting to get slightly concerned about what the editor would say if I returned from Mongolia without the "money shot," as I can guarantee you it would have all somehow boiled down to being my fault. As I'm sure you can imagine, the pressures on angling journalists are tremendous. Something had to change. So while Deke and Bill went off with Charlie, Carl, and the rest of the crew to fish the upper river and spend a night in the top camp, Dan and I headed back downstream. We needed to change the batting order, and, secretly, I suspected that one of my compadres had probably left a bum fly at the monastery and we were all being punished for it. And indeed, not one hour after we parted ways, my suspicions were

confirmed. Dan had seen a likely looking slough mouth on our way upstream, so we decided to give it a lash on the way back down. As he cast his way down the run, working his fly along the seam of the cut bank and down past the slough mouth, a huge taimen suddenly boiled on the offering—and missed! Obviously, this was no ten-pounder, and, luckily, it stayed around to fight. Dan could now see the fish clearly, and a few casts later, not forty feet from where we stood, his fly went down in a huge and spectacular explosion of water, and this monster taimen was eventually landed. The fish was massive—over fifty inches, with a great green head and big wide shoulders tapering down to the taimenesque red tail and large adipose fin. It looked like an entirely different animal than the smaller ones we'd been catching, and topping off the whole affair, the sun even came out for photos.

Clearly, I had been a victim of some kind of bad vibe coming off Deke and Bill, since Dan had nailed the big one and I had put what I hoped would be a cover shot safely in the can on the same afternoon that we bade those two ne'er-do-wells a fond farewell. However, not even thirty-six hours had elapsed before I was forced to rethink this position. As it turned out, first thing the next morning, Bill connected with an over fifty-inch trophy, and later in the day, Deke landed one in the mid-forties. In addition, later that afternoon, Bill further engaged in an epic twenty-minute struggle with what Deke, Bill, and Carl all swore was a sixty-inch levi-

athan that came unbuttoned right at the boat. This day, JD also had a huge and highly aggressive fish charge his fly close enough to the boat that he was actually splashed by the missed attempt. He was apparently so shaken by the experience that when Charlie prompted him to flick his fly back into the water, he responded, "I'm not so sure I want to!"

It was an absolutely outstanding two days of taimen fishing that resulted not only in true trophies brought to hand, but also in a couple epic tales of the ones that got away—and we all know how the latter have the greater potential to improve over time. So despite the obvious character flaw that forces me to immediately assign blame to the innocent, it seemed that the river gods had chosen to smile upon all of our fortunes anyway, finally granting us our wishes and allowing us the most rare and exotic opportunities to briefly hold, admire, photograph, and otherwise get up close and personal with several of their most spectacular daughters. And that, my friends, is just one of the reasons you don't leave just any old crappy fly at the Dayan Derkh Monastery.

Indeed, our entire week at the Eg-Urr camp seemed to be charmed with nothing but good fortune. In addition to an amiable and stalwart group of anglers and guides, we were also treated to the company of a diverse and interesting collection of folks, beginning with Puji himself, Jeff's original guide, and the Mongolian camp staff who befriended us and made certain every aspect of our stay was perfect. In addition, this week we concurrently had a small international taimen summit going on in camp composed of the following distinguished delegates: Jeffery Liebert of the International Finance Corporation; Gantula, an honest to goodness Buddhist monk (complete with traditional robe and beads); Betsy Gaines-Quammen, director of the Tributary Fund; Erdenbat Eldevochir, director of the Taimen Conservation Fund; Suddeep Chandra, professor of limnology, University of Nevada, Reno; and Zeb Hogan, research biologist, University of Wisconsin, Madison.

Together with Dan Vermillion of Sweetwater Travel and its angling clients, this eclectic and international group of people represented the unlikely convergence of diverse interests united here for the common purpose of conserving these unique fish and their habitat. Finally, in confirmation of the fact that this was indeed a highly important gathering, there was even a mini press gallery in attendance in the form of Peter Wonacott, a reporter from the *Wall Street Journal*. In a befitting conclusion to this important summit and angling trip, on our last night in camp we were held spellbound by exotic strains of Mongolian throat singing and folk music performed by a group of local artists resplendent in full traditional regalia.

I told you at the outset that a fishing trip to Mongolia was anything but normal, didn't I? I'd often heard that this region of Mongolia closely resembles parts of Montana. And, while I haven't spent any amount of time in that fair state, somehow the comparison is hard for me to imagine. The images of Mongolia that now often drift through my mind go something like this. I see the early morning frost glittering off the white sides of the *gers* and the smoke rising from their chimneys and hanging low in the air like fog. I see hillsides covered in unbroken forests of birch and larch, on fire with the colors of their fall foliage, and the broad, clear waters of the Urr River winding through them. I see the magnificent sight of a large herd of horses thundering along the riverbank in spectacular late afternoon light and the smiling faces of the four men and women driving them, mounted on wooden saddles, riding down to meet us. I see the surprised look on the face of the wolf that jumped into the river and swam across it, right in front of our speeding jet boat, and the large flock of enormous vultures that circled above the riverbank one afternoon. Of course, I see taimen and lenok, too, just released, suspended as if in midair in the ultra-clear waters of the Urr. And, believe it or not, I see the large taimen that swam into camp as we stood on the riverbank waiting for our helicopter ride home. No kidding—it happened for us too. For whatever reason,

no one cast to this fish, but rather, we just watched in disbelief as it slowly swam upstream and eventually out of sight. I just don't know how much of that I'm likely to see when I get around to going to Montana.

Finally, to end this tale in the same peculiar way it started, I would beseech you to go and gaze in wonder upon the fly rods stored in the corners of your closets. For whether made of graphite, or bamboo, or anything in between, each is nothing less than a bona fide magic wand. If you let them, they'll allow you to "slip the surly bonds of earth," in the words of poet John Gillespie Magee, and hold gracefully ethereal loops of fly line in the air, which ultimately joins you to the universal life force of all wild things through the species they connect you with. And what's more, if you let them, they'll also take you to the very edges of the earth, opening up magical worlds of unimaginable beauty, ancient cultures, modern science, and indescribably enriching relationships and life experiences that most certainly would otherwise be left unseen and unknown. Think I'm nuts? Follow your fly rod to Mongolia and you'll see what I mean.

155

CHAPTER 10

Romancing the Rio Santa Cruz

Atlantic Steelhead: Santa Cruz, Argentina

We were just inches from a clean getaway. After months of planning, scheming, and dreaming, and through countless conversations, e-mails, and a series of unlikely yet serendipitous connections, we were teetering on the precipice of just having successfully planned and executed the steelheading equivalent of the perfect crime. In many ways, it was a crime of passion, but whatever the case, this one had it all: intrigue, politics, adventure and discovery, adversity and triumph, brushes with the law, and mysterious, dark-eyed chicas, a bittersweet ending, and, of course, plenty of booze, smokes, and rock and roll. And that the fish and fishing involved were spectacular as well should by now be tacitly understood.

Indeed, this was an angling expedition for the ages, one that would be difficult to duplicate anywhere in the world and a fishing trip against which all others would henceforth be measured. And, not only were we on the verge of pulling it off flawlessly, but in a style only befitting such a grand and ambitious caper. But then, on the penultimate day of a two week long expedition, the river completely and utterly blew out on us. Just like that, it went from absolutely perfect to absolutely unfishable overnight. It was as if the clock had simply run out, the whistle had blown, and the river herself had just slammed the doors right shut. We had been shown enough.

At nightfall of the previous day, we had driven down to the very run we intended to fish first thing the next morning just to case it out. That night, water conditions were still ideal, and everything was ticking along just fine. But more to the point, for the very first time in twelve days of covering some 150 fantastic miles of virgin river, we had also finally reached a piece of known water, and an allegedly spectacular one at that. So good, in fact, that Mario, one of the very few anglers who had been here before, not only predicted we would hook

Rio Santa Cruz, Argentina

smug and content, silently congratulating ourselves in advance for the obvious victory at hand.

In retrospect, we probably should have recognized the mere notion of "guaranteed steelhead" and the act of premature self-congratulation as clear signs of impending disaster, but remember, at that point, we were still golden—untouchable. After all, led by Vern Olson of Camano Island, Washington, and Mario Zwetzig of Piedra Buena, Argentina, our crew of one American, two Canadians, and seven Argentinos had just completed the first ever angling survey of the agua incognita of the Rio Santa Cruz, home to arguably the most distinctive run of steelhead in the entire world. Ergo, in our minds at least, it followed logically that we had just become one of the most distinctive groups of steelheaders in the entire world. No matter who or what would follow, as far as this river and her steelhead were concerned, the fact would remain in perpetuity that we'd been the first. And while being first wasn't our primary motivation, frankly, I'd be lying like a politician if I told you that we didn't think that was pretty damn cool nonetheless.

Flowing from high in the Andean cordillera, the Rio Santa Cruz is born of two massive lakes: Lago Viedma and Lago Argentino. Protected by a fortress of impossibly jagged peaks and surrounded by vast fields of permanent ice, the latter is also home to the spectacular Perito Moreno Glacier, a UNESCO-designated World Heritage Site. From here, near the Chilean border, this wild river runs eastward, free and undisturbed, through

steelhead, he absolutely guaranteed it. And despite the fact that he relayed this to us in Spanish, we unequivocally understood that as long as we were breathing, tomorrow would just be a question of how big and how many, and we had neither reason nor desire to doubt him. So, in full expectation of waking up to what Vern would call a "slugfest," as well as the most fitting end to the most perfect fishing trip ever, we went to bed

some 250 miles of the vast, windswept Patagonian steppe, its glacially tinted waters tracing an incongruously electric blue ribbon of current across the rolling brown, semiarid plains of southern Argentina before spilling into the Atlantic at Puerto Santa Cruz. It is the second largest river system in southern Patagonia and home to the only scientifically documented run of anadromous rainbow trout, or steelhead, in Argentina, and more significant, the one and only documented case of true Atlantic-run steelhead anywhere.

Having successfully surveyed this special river from its headwaters right down to the outer edges of the known water, we had largely fulfilled our mission of angling exploration. Nonetheless, sleeping on guaranteed steelhead and waking up to a guaranteed skunk was still a considerable psychological drop. However, we somehow found the grace to make the only appropriate response to our spectacular rebuff. First, we swiftly resigned ourselves to our fate. (Okay, there was a brief bout of whining and feeling sorry for ourselves.) And then, we kicked back with a force, flavor, and indeed grandeur only possible in Argentina. We threw a whole *cordero* (lamb) on the *asado* (barbeque), broke out the truco cards (gaucho poker), and spent the entire day calling each other's bluffs, recounting our recent days of angling glory, and reveling in the camaraderie of our newly forged international fly-fishing fraternity. We spoke of friends, family, flies, and fishing, and of the sweet satisfaction in solving the myriad mysteries

Rio Santa Cruz, Argentina

of steelhead in both the northern and southern hemispheres. We made fishing plans and promises for the future. We feasted on appetizers of salads and sizzling hot *chorizos*, as strains of Santana, Frankenreiter, and Argentinean folklore further sweetened our surroundings. And finally, over the long and happy hours it took our *cordero* to crisp to an Argentinean standard of *asador-eal* perfection (and trust me, this is worlds

beneath what now appeared to be massive, swirling currents of *café con leche*. Now it might have been the Malbec, but our mood had lifted considerably, and Vern and I actually started thinking we'd figured something out. Because as far as the Rio Santa Cruz was concerned, well, let's just say she'd toyed with us like this before.

FIRST ENCOUNTER

In fact, it was during our initial flirtation with this river over a year prior to this current episode that she'd pulled sort of a similar stunt, albeit on a far grander scale. Like the few other diehard foreign steelheaders before us, we'd been attracted to her by stories of an exotic southern beauty rumored to have the best set of steelhead south of the North Umpqua, so to speak—and Atlantic-run steelhead to boot. Therefore, at the end of a trip to the sea-trout rivers of southern Patagonia, we stopped in for a quick peek, if only to confirm or deny for ourselves the existence of such fabled charms. But in a stroke of spectacularly bad luck and timing, this was also the year that the glacial ice dam finally collapsed. And yes, this is as catastrophic to river conditions as it sounds.

As we were to learn, the advancing Perito Moreno glacier periodically cuts off one entire arm of massive Lago Argentino. Inevitably, the rising waters behind this huge wall of ice cause it to fail, whereupon with a great crack and a bang, jillions upon jillions of gallons

Atlantic Steelhead,
Rio Santa Cruz, Argentina

160

apart from just another weenie roast), we slowly but surely got hammered on Quilmes beer and gallons of the world's finest Malbec. Viva Argentina.

Thus, from outside our small cabin at Estancia San Ramon, we slowly began to regain some perspective, and our world gradually came back into focus. Around us, the ever-present wind blew across the dusty brown southern Patagonian plains, which seemed to ramble off infinitely in all directions. And before us, the Rio Santa Cruz did her best to blend into the brown, coyly cruising on by toward the Atlantic, offering no excuses for once again shrouding her secrets and her steelhead

of silty, turbid, glacial puke are suddenly released, with no place else to go but straight down the Rio Santa Cruz. Just based on the connotation of the term "glacial speed," you can imagine that this is not an everyday occurrence. In fact, we could have shown up here any time within the previous sixteen years and left completely ignorant of the existence of this random geophysical phenomenon. That year, though, with sixteen years worth of pent up glacial goo behind it, the dam broke on March 13, 2004, at precisely 7:09 p.m., just twenty-six days before our arrival.

Our first date with the Rio Santa Cruz, therefore, was made even more awkward than what one might normally expect from first-time jitters. Still retaining a good deal of water, she was definitely bloated and looked more than just a little surly, hardly in the best mood or shape to accommodate our desires. Glacial silt had reduced visibility to the point that we could hardly see down past her very top button, and, in fact, we found her to be just barely fishable. Nonetheless, hosted by outfitter Mariano Soler and chaperoned by local guides Piti Chaparro and Pablo Destafano, we set out to try our luck in the waters around the small town of Piedra Buena. However inopportune our timing, we had come all the way down to southern Patagonia for this, and we had to take a shot. So under these difficult conditions, for three full days, Joe, Rich, Vern, and I threw whatever piscatorial patience and charm we could muster at the Rio Santa Cruz to see just how far we could get.

We probed run after swollen run with determination and long double-handed rods, dangling our prettiest flies and swinging them as deeply and slowly as possible. Sensitive to the circumstances, we were gentle but persistent. But despite our prolonged and repeated appeals, the Santa Cruz remained aloof, and for all our attempts, only allowed us to lay our hands on two and a half fish over our entire three-day campaign. That said, when she did give in, we found her steelhead to be beautifully firm, taut, and shapely—and real. Atlantic steelhead! The first was a feisty, nickel-bright hen of about eight pounds, yielded to Vern. The second was an impressive sixteen-pound buck, as shiny and strong as the first that again accepted an offering from that old steelhead charmer Vern. The half (actually caught between the first and second) was a small yet equally brilliant beauty seduced to the fly by Joe and one that was essentially in hand. However, as I ran to grab the camera, Joe experienced an unfortunate, premature release.

Now under normal circumstances, even in steelheading, four rods, three days, and two and a half fish would hardly be cause for a serious second glance. But our circumstances here were hardly normal. You will recall there was that little dam incident. Also, we found this lower section of the river to be uninspiring at best, composed mostly of soft, muddy, clay-like banks sometimes with a sprinkling of small gravel. In fact, fishing here often seemed more like fishing the muddy shores

of a large lake rather than any steelhead stream we'd known. On the positive side, we were able to confirm for ourselves the very existence of these fish, and the few we saw were absolutely brilliant—blindingly bright, strong, and solid. They were at least equal in every important respect to the finest and freshest of their summer-run North American cousins.

But perhaps most compelling was the fact that we had glimpsed a very young steelhead fishery, which these days is a unique situation in itself. It seemed odd to us that virtually all the fishermen were still using single-handed rods on a river that would be considered massive by British Columbia standards. And curiously, their efforts were still exclusively focused on just a very short stretch of a very long river. So even in her less than perfect state, the Rio Santa Cruz had played us perfectly. She'd shown us just enough to engage our interest, while still leaving plenty for our fertile imaginations. Let's face it—we've all had cheap thrills with those really quick and easy rivers in the short term, but you've got to admit that invariably, their appeal tends to fade just as fast. The Santa Cruz, on the other hand, was no such pushover.

ABSENCE MAKES THE HEART GROW FONDER

Over the months that followed, the idea of getting to know this river more intimately just kept looming larger and larger in our minds, and definitely not for the lack of some very worthy attractions closer to home. In fact, Vern and I worked hard to keep ourselves well distracted. We chased summer runs on the Skeena, Bulkley, and Nass. We chased winter runs on the Hoh, Skagit, and Sauk. Yet on each outing and even in the presence of these gorgeous rivers, virtually all we could talk about was the Rio Santa Cruz.

So based on just three days prior knowledge and from thousands of miles away, this exotic and mysterious river worked her spell, and you could safely say we became completely obsessed. We'd caught glimpses of her fine Atlantic steelhead and knew that once they got past the tidal portions of the river, they went unmolested, a fact that we had a real hard time getting our heads around. And, in short, it simply drove us stark raving nuts fantasizing about the untold piscatorial pleasures the virgin stretches of this 250-mile river might hold.

Now, in order to truly understand the situation that was unfolding, the first thing you need know about my buddy Vern is that he's absolutely passionate about steelhead. And where these fish are concerned, he thinks big: big fish, big rods, big flies, big ideas. The second thing is, he follows through, and never in half measures. So, in the course of one of our obsession sessions, when he raised the notion of shipping jet boats from Seattle to Puerto Santa Cruz, not only did I know this wasn't just idle chatter, I also knew that he was truly sick for the Rio Santa Cruz and was going back at

Opposite page:
Rio Santa Cruz, Argentina

163

all costs. When he threatened once to go without me, that's when I knew I had it just as bad.

So the game was on, and we went at it with as much fury as you'd expect from a couple of obsessed suitors. Everything you could possibly glean about the Rio Santa Cruz from Seattle and Vancouver, we gleaned. We Googled her and read virtually every word any angler had ever posted about her in both English and Spanish. We looked at every low-res inch of her on Internet satellite sites, and from the fuzzy blue lines imagined the most spectacular steelhead runs possible. We spoke to everyone we knew who had been anywhere on or near the Santa Cruz, and even tracked down strangers who claimed some knowledge of the river. We heard tales from those who knew her, and those who said they knew her, and we got some obviously factual and helpful accounts, but others that were equally blatant fabrications. We were encouraged by some in our quest, yet actively discouraged by others. And finally, having turned over all the stones we possibly could from the Pacific Northwest, we deployed our secret southern weapon—Juan Luis Ariztegui, our man on the ground in Argentina.

Juan had steered both Vern and me around that country before on separate occasions, and we trusted him implicitly. So we told our Argentinean agent we wanted to start at the very top of the river, out of the small town of El Calafate, and go all the way downstream, right back to Piedra Buena. We would need a four-wheel-drive truck big enough for the three of us and our gear, with trailer hitch;

a trailer; a boat with an outboard motor (preferably a jet); accommodations along the entire river (anything except tents); information on river access (specific, eye-witnessed spots); and a couple of cases of the best *vino tinto* he could find (Argentinean of course). As simple as all that might have just sounded, in reality, it was next to impossible. Jet boats behind four-wheel drive trucks, gas stations, and roadside motels just do not exist in abundance in the remote and sparsely settled regions of southern Patagonia. Luckily though, there is no shortage of great red wine.

As expected, Juan's immediate response was, "No problem guys! I'm starting on this right now. Look forward to seeing you." And although we relayed the idea of a hard-ass, no frills, do-it-yourself river journey across the wilds of southern Patagonia from the Andes to the Atlantic, Juan further suggested that at the end of it all, we could drive from Piedra Buena back to Buenos Aires (some 1,500 miles) just to party for a few days. Obviously, he was undaunted by our little proposition. So day by day, week by week, our plan began falling into place. But just days before Vern and I were to leave for our long anticipated second engagement with the Rio Santa Cruz, one minor detail remained unresolved: we still didn't have a boat. At this stage in the game, though, it was too late to change course. The juggernaut we'd created was unstoppable.

Juan had left Buenos Aires and was already in Patagonia, feverishly working on our little boat problem. I had left Vancouver for Islamorada to attend a friend's birthday celebration on my way to Buenos Aires. Our buddy Jim Allen, a steelhead guide from Kispiox, British Columbia, who had just finished his trout-guiding season in Chile, had left Coyhaique bound for El Calafate to meet us. Vern was still sweating it out in Seattle, but with full intentions to leave. Then, on the eve of his departure, we had a significant and truly serendipitous breakthrough. Mario Zwetzig phoned back. And, after a short meeting with our man Juan in Rio Gallegos, the entire face of the trip we had planned for months instantly transformed itself into something we'd never imagined.

Mario is an Argentinean angling guide extraordinaire who's specialties cover some of the country's most interesting fishing: dorado in northern Argentina, sea trout in the Rio Gallegos, and, of course, steelhead in the Rio Santa Cruz. As a local Piedra Buena guide, he's the one we had attempted to contact in our search for information and a boat, but as he was away guiding, we just hadn't heard back from him. Finally, though, he contacted Juan, and to make a long story short, Mario and crew—all associated with Loop Tackle in Argentina—decided on the spot to join our expedition. Along with Mario, the Loop crew included Claudio Martin and Diego Coscia, aka "Pollo," sea-trout guides who had just ended their season, and Gabriel Tournour, the lodge manager and business partner in Loop's Las Buitreras Lodge on the Rio Gallegos. In addition, the father and son duo of Alberto and Albert Zwetzig (brother and nephew of Mario, respectively) would come along to provide support.

Opposite page:
Rio Santa Cruz, Argentina

165

This last-minute collaboration of forces with "Team Loop Argentina" couldn't have been more perfect. First, we'd met Gabriel, Claudio, and Pollo the year prior at Las Buitreras and looked forward to again sharing their company and angling prowess. Also, Mario knew the peculiarities of fishing for these southern steelhead like no other, and combined with our ideas and experiences from British Columbia and the Pacific Northwest, we were confident that the Rio Santa Cruz didn't stand a chance. And last but not least, they had boats! So literally overnight we went from no boat to two boats, from two trucks to four, from three anglers to six, and from the prospect of drinking our wine with peanut butter sandwiches to having a crew who would actually cook. Our rendezvous with the Rio Santa Cruz was indeed looking more and more like a date with destiny.

On this day, at long last, we could finally say we woke up beside our beloved Rio Santa Cruz again, meeting the crimson blush of the early morning sun near her headwaters in the quaint mountain village of El Calafate. For the next fourteen sunrises, instead of "good morning," it was hearty and repeated rounds of "*Como amaneciste?*" from Mario, to the point that this became the rallying cry for our expedition. And despite the fact that our first sunrise here found Team Loop Argentina and Team North American "Extranjeros" (plus Juan) a little weary and hung over from our *asado*/strategy session the night before, we were more than ready to rock at sunrise. We had just one last necessary stop to make before our long anticipated reunion with the river, but in doing so, found out that this second date came complete with a thorough interrogation from a suspicious and overprotective father in the form of the Argentinean river authorities. Indeed, Papa Prefectura had a few questions for us before they'd let us out on our own with their lovely river—three excruciating hours' worth, to be exact, which included an unexpectedly close examination of our equipment. Finally, though, we convinced them of our honorable intentions, were begrudgingly determined to be river worthy, and with their blessings thus won, we rushed to the river to take advantage of what was left in the day, and to finally lay our eyes on the Rio Santa Cruz again for the first time in over a year. After all this, as you might have expected, we were somewhat overwhelmed by what we found. This day, *el viento loco*, the infamous winds of Patagonia, blew in characteristically impressive fashion, thrashing the surface of the river into a confusing and illegible tableau of conflicting currents. Casting was obviously going to be a challenge, but in these conditions, reading water was virtually impossible. Also, we expected that, like most rivers, the Santa Cruz would start small and grow bigger as she moved toward the sea but instead learned that this river starts big and then gets bigger still. Even here near the outflow of Lago Argentino at the Charles Fuhr bridge, she looked to be almost a quarter-mile wide.

I told you the Santa Cruz was no pushover, and our formidable challenge for the next two weeks was clearly and obviously laid before us. We faced a huge, unreadable river whipped by winds strong enough for you to actually lean into without falling, and our task was to find steelhead in stretches no one was even sure these fish reached. As we all know, however, love is blind, and no doubt heavily influenced by our previous year's experience, we noticed right away that the Rio Santa Cruz actually cleans up very nicely indeed. Sure, she was a little windy, and not quite as petite as we'd imagined, but nonetheless, this year, we saw that she had sufficient clarity, and that's all the encouragement we needed.

For team North America, our approach to solving the Santa Cruz was based largely on experiences with summer runs from back home. As for likely places, there were two main elements at the top of our list. The first was defined structure—simply put, rocks, ranging from defined gravel bars and breaks, right through to big boulder gardens with nice greasy slicks. In the small "known" section of the lower river around Piedra Buena, rocks were nonexistent (which is ironic, as "Piedra Buena" translates into "good" or "nice rock"). Second, we planned to focus on tributaries, speculating that at least one or all of those we saw on the maps would be important spawning areas that steelhead would be homing in on. Furthermore, considering they weren't glacial in origin, we also hoped that one or all of these would be clear-water streams. Team Argentina's focus, on the

other hand, was primarily on perfect water depth and speed. In the absence of defined structure, these factors are the key to success in the lower river, so perhaps not too surprising, Mario proved to be an uncanny master at reading this type of water. In fact, it seemed he could do this even when it was so windy you could swear the river was flowing upstream.

Lake trout, Rio Santa Cruz, Argentina

Rio Santa Cruz, Argentina

THE UPPER RIVER

Based in Calafate, we explored the upper river for the next five days, moving progressively downstream. Unfortunately, the Rio Bote confluence didn't pan out quite the way we'd hoped, as it turned out to be but a mere trickle of a stream, draining meekly into the Santa Cruz in a broad, undefined, and uninspiring area of gradually sloping muddy banks. Indeed, we encountered far broader, clay-banked runs in the upper river than we'd expected to, and in good natured disrespect, Vern and I started to refer to these areas as "Piedra Buena water." Around the Rio Bote, though, we were doubly deflated, as our research had indicated that it was the largest tributary we would encounter, so we had come here with high hopes. Sarcasm aside, we fished all the Piedra Buena water, including that around the Rio Bote, with open minds, at first, mostly because Mario insisted that we do so, but later because we began to understand why. On day one, we saw our first such example, as Mario hooked and landed the very first steelhead of our trip just below this uninspiring little stream.

We were absolutely elated. The first fish of any trip is always exciting, but this one was particularly special, as it was undeniable confirmation of our unscientific guess that there would be steelhead in the upper river at this time of year. Considering we had more than 150 miles to go, this was a good thing to know. Early on, we also began to encounter the rocky runs we'd come up here hoping to find, and the first serious structure (and to our eyes, really fishy looking water) we'd seen anywhere on the Santa Cruz. Mario, however, was initially somewhat less than impressed. In fact, at the first boulder garden we found, he didn't even want to stop! We insisted he fish "our kind of water" as well, though, and as days passed, he gradually warmed up to the idea.

In terms of her steelhead, the Santa Cruz also progressively became more accommodating as days passed. The day after Mario's first fish, she gave up another, and also provided us with a few healthy grabs that didn't always result in landed steelhead but were undeniable indications of their presence. And quite sincerely, to us, that was almost as good. As my friend and British Columbia steelhead guide Geoff Straight would say, "the tug is the drug," and on this particular trip, this couldn't have been closer to the truth. That we all wanted to catch fish was of course a given. However, for this trip, the excitement of exploration and discovery seemed in everyone's minds at least as appealing as actual fish in hand. Also, considering we had very little time to cover a lot of river, we didn't really linger in any given spot. It was more important for us to find spots and get to know as much of the river as possible rather than try and run up the numbers. So, the initial rhythm of our dance with the Santa Cruz was torrid, to say the least. We'd book down runs at double or triple normal speed, and most often after a landed fish or an undeniable grab, check off the run as good and move on to find the next.

For boating, the Santa Cruz was forgiving, even relaxing to be on. Flowing through rolling, relatively flat terrain, she is a generous, sweeping river, with no really difficult water to speak of. In fact, never once in our relationship did she give us any anxiety nor needless displays of drama by throwing irrational, whitewater fits. Periodically, she was simply spectacular, showing us expansive, swirling bends along stunningly sheer sandstone cliffs sculpted into other worldly shapes and spires that reflected off her deep turquoise waters like fleeting, dancing sheets of gold leaf. At other times, she

was more muted—pale icy blue, meandering though desert-like sand dunes and dry rolling hills blanketed with thorny, scrubby *mata negras* and sparse tufts of hardy grasses that partially covered the sandy brown landscape like a three-day growth of beard. Sometimes, condors soared high overhead on the thermals of *viento loco*, while exotic southern geese and ducks skimmed along closer to the earth. And everywhere around us, small groups of guanacos and nandus (rheas) periodically populated the arid, treeless, exotic landscape.

At the end of our fifth full day, we found the most interesting stretch of water we would see on the entire upper river. "Sweet Caroline," as this run came to be known, is a long stretch of soft water over two-hundred yards long, beginning just before and continuing around a sweeping left-hand bend. At the head, the current pushes into a heavy, fast flow that hugs a high bank on the opposite side, while inside the main seam is a wide greasy slick, studded with big boulders and with a bottom of rocks from baseball to bowling ball size. It simply had steelhead written all over it. When we first got there, though, it also had a gale blowing straight across it, making the idea of casting into it a mere fantasy. For the moment, all we could do was look, and it would be a while before we could touch.

When we did, though, Sweet Caroline produced. We consistently got grabs throughout the run and landed fish at the top, middle, and bottom, and on everything from big, deeply sunk flies fished off heavy tips right up to a Lady Caroline Spey fly hung in the surface film off a floating line (hence the name of the run). In fact, the only thing that didn't work was a skated dry, although Jimmy gave it a good long attempt one afternoon. And while there seemed to be no reason why the dry wouldn't produce here, you've got to admit that the nickname "Sweet Bomber" wouldn't have had quite as nice a ring to it. Also, in a complete surprise, one afternoon Sweet Caroline gave up a lake trout of close to twenty pounds that took a black General Practitioner again, fished high off a floating line. All told it was exactly the kind of run we'd come here hoping to find, and, in addition, it was the run that made Mario a true believer in the quality of these rocky, and to him, overly shallow runs.

ADVENTURE LODGING AT ESTANCIA ENRIQUETTA

By this point, the commute by road back to Calafate was taking us over an hour and a half, so we were reluctantly forced to leave the charms and comforts of town and venture into the realm of what Juan liked to call "adventure lodging." And he knew of what he spoke, since over the course of the first five days, while we were on the river fishing, our advance team (namely Juan) had been driving the rough and dusty back roads of Patagonia, finding every possible river access while also keeping an eye out for any possible place to which we could relocate. The region between Calafate and Piedra Buena is a vast, seemingly uninhabited stretch of one sprawling estancia after another. In fact, over our entire fourteen days on the river, we saw only one other human being, a lone gaucho riding along with a posse of herding dogs. Nonetheless, each day, Juan magically managed to find and check out every possible river access, which often involved crossing private property through locked gates. Invariably, though, he returned with permission, as well as the keys required to open any and all of the locked gates along the way, and usually, he managed to get himself a free lunch in the process. How he found anyone out there remains a mystery, but that's our Juan. So not too surprising, he had found us a place to stay on Estancia Enriquetta, a long unused estancia house with no running water and powered only by a small gas generator: adventure-lodging Patagonia at its finest.

Getting out of Calafate, though, wasn't quite as easy. Adventure lodging also meant self-sufficiency in food and fuel, so we spent the better part of an entire day packing our things and buying supplies, which included filling two forty-five gallon drums of fuel to keep everything going until we reached Piedra Buena. And since no adventure is complete without a little drama and adversity, this day, that's exactly what we got. It all started quite innocently, when in the course of filling everything up with fuel, the attendant mistakenly filled Jim's truck up with diesel fuel instead of gasoline. And from this little incident, our day rapidly

unraveled into a mind-boggling disaster of international proportions. Occurring across a significant language barrier, heated debates with the gas jockeys somehow led to a screaming match with a "tow truck driver" (a guy with a pickup and a rope) that took place in broad daylight on the town's main boulevard and was eventually mediated by a police officer who happened by at an opportune moment. Finally, several hours and one partially torn biceps tendon later (don't even ask), the serial absurdities subsided, and the little town of Calafate became but a dusty reflection in the rearview mirror as we bounced our way down the rutted dirt road, bound for our new digs at Enriquetta.

Despite the wasted fishing day, from the relative safety of our little bunk house at Enriquetta, we determined that we were indeed ahead of schedule. So from this new base, situated about a third of the way down the river, we gave ourselves a respite from fishing at breakneck speed and even took the luxury of going back upstream, deciding to slow down and spend some quality time at the places we found most interesting. And as luck would have it, the area we accessed from Enriquetta held the most interesting water, as well as the best and most pleasant period of fishing we enjoyed on the entire river.

At the top of this stretch was Sweet Caroline. We fished there on two more occasions, and we left that run with a perfect record. That is, although we went through that water more times than any other, we never struck out, catching at least one fish (and most often many more) every time we visited. It was also the only run that gave up fish consistently on a dry line, and the site where Jim caught one of the biggest fish of the trip, a buck of about thirty-seven inches.

Downstream of Enriquetta, we fished around another very small tributary coming in on river left, and while it was Piedra Buena water, we managed to hit a few nice fish there. By this time we weren't as biased against this type of water, and from watching and listening to Mario, had started to recognize and learn some of the subtle breaks and features he was reading. So as we worked our way down this section for the next five days, we fished all the interesting holding water from muddy clay banks to rocky runs and everything in between, and there was a lot of it to go around. And not only did much of this water hold fish, we were also hooking and landing them more consistently. In fact, all five days we spent on this stretch were multiple-fish days. That would be an admirable stat even when fishing known and famous steelhead rivers. For exploratory steelheading, it was simply incredible.

Our evenings at the bunkhouse in Enriquetta were also among the most enjoyable times of this trip. Here, we found the truco cards, learned to bluff like real gauchos, and got addicted to the game. And on one evening we were treated to one of the most uniquely authentic Patagonian meals any of us are ever likely to eat— *empanadas of nandu* (rhea) followed by a main course of *nandu milanesa,* paired of course with a rich red Malbec. It turns out that on the way home that evening, one particularly unlucky *nandu* had happened to run in front of Team Argentina's truck and met a somewhat undignified demise. The team wisely collected it, kept it well hidden, and then served it to us in the form of the two traditional Argentinean dishes, all the while doing their best not to burst out laughing. Nonetheless, the *nandu* was delicious, and in addition to the meal and the joke, it also provided an abundance of great tying material. (Just check out the price of one rhea feather next time you're in a fly shop.) In fact, were we not men of such high moral standard, we would have gone well out of our way to run over another one the next night.

MAGIC BUSH

After five such fun-filled nights and days at Enriquetta, however, we had again reached our downstream limit, and reluctantly needed to move on. Luckily, we still had our own fuel. At this point the river had started to widen out substantially, and rocky runs were no longer to be found. As we were now approaching the lower end of the river, the entire landscape was more reminiscent of the coastal region around Piedra Buena. This fact notwithstanding, just before we reached our final stop at Estancia San Ramon, we found the run that produced the most and biggest fish in the shortest period of time in our entire trip.

Magic Bush was a real sleeper, outwardly looking like typical, featureless Piedra Buena water. Indeed, the most obvious feature here was a big thorny bush situated right down at the water, and left to our own devices, we might have missed it altogether and floated right on past. But Mario homed in on it like a pointer on a pheasant, and it soon became obvious why. Initially, I went up to the head of the run, Mario started just above the bush, and Vern went in below. And on this very first pass, as he got even with the bush, Mario hit a beautiful, unbelievably hot steelhead of about fifteen pounds that took most of his backing, jumping, and greyhounding across the surface in spectacular fashion. It took about fifteen minutes to land, and was probably the hottest fish hooked on the entire trip. Over just the next hour and a half or so, the action got hot and heavy. Between Vern and Mario, five more explosive fish were hooked and two of them landed, all right beside or just down past that bush. Mario officially named this run Skagit Minnow for the fly he caught the first fish on, but we're sticking to Magic Bush.

Finally, with daylight waning, we floated down into Estancia San Ramon. Still a good day's run from Piedra Buena by boat, this area represents the very upper reaches of the known water of the lower Santa Cruz, so in effect, our days of pure exploration were over. But even at that, Mario was probably one of the very few people with any prior experience whatsoever this far upriver and there was still a lot of new water in this area we hoped to check out. And while it was late in the

173

Rio Santa Cruz, Argentina

174

Hasta la proxima vez, mi amor : Until next time, my love

So, our whirlwind romance with the Rio Santa Cruz had finally come to an end. For two full weeks though and over 150 miles, she'd shown us the time of our lives. We covered her from top to bottom, and she had given us steelhead from previously unexplored water every single day. Initially, therefore, we were really quite confused (maybe even a little hurt) by what now appeared to be a very abrupt change of heart. She'd been so cool up until now. Could it have been something we said?

But then Vern provided an explanation, reasoning that this blowout wasn't a rejection at all, but just her way of slowing things down a bit. His take was that the river wasn't quite ready to give it all up just yet. She'd shown us plenty for now, and if we wanted more, well, we'd just have to come back. Fair enough, for although it was prolonged, this really was only our second date. And, we already knew this river wasn't easy. So although she didn't give us the big happy ending we'd expected, she wasn't shutting us out, just making sure we'd come back by saving it for another time. After all, this ploy had worked on us once before. So maybe Vern was right: this wasn't a refusal, but rather, an invitation to a more meaningful and longer-term affair. Now again, it might have been the Malbec, but whatever the case, this was certainly a most beautiful way to think. Ain't love (and steelheading) grand?

day, Mario couldn't wait to show us the run he'd told us so much about already, so we drove down at dusk to check it out. Like Magic Bush, this was another very subtle piece of water, but we were more educated now, and especially after Mario's stories, we were more than anxious to get a crack at her the following morning. Of course, you already know what happened overnight.

AFTERWORD

WHERE ARE WE GOING NEXT?

Whether it's just the pool around the bend, or the next river, stream, saltwater flat, country, continent, or even species, the ever-seeking soul of the fly fisher seems always to have an eye on the next cast, the next discovery, and the next adventure. And, while our world seems to shrink rapidly before our eyes in so many ways, the world of adventure fly fishing and of fly fishing in general seems at this point in time to be exploding and flourishing as never before.

Historically speaking, it wasn't all too long ago in my home province of British Columbia that common knowledge stated that Pacific salmon and even steelhead couldn't be caught with flies. And, while on some days, it can sometimes still seem that way to me, today fly anglers are catching Pacific salmon all the way from salt to stream as a matter of course, and British Columbia steelhead are one of the dream species for fly fishers the

world over. A more contemporary example of a similar situation is the sleek and powerful milkfish found on the tropical saltwater flats. Like bonefish that grow to the size of tarpon with the strength and fighting characteristics of both, milkfish are algae feeders, and therefore, until fairly recently, it was commonly held that they couldn't be caught on flies. Now, they are the marquis game fish of the Seychelles, and fly anglers travel to that remote tropical paradise just to fish for them.

Today, if we can get within casting distance, nothing that swims is safe from the imagination and determination of the modern fly fisher. Whether it's mako shark in California, marlin off the Galapagos, halibut in Alaska, taimen in Mongolia (or sea-run taimen on the Sakhalin Islands for that matter), sea-run Arctic Char in the Canadian high Arctic, monster bones in New Caledonia, or giant snakehead and kassop kit in Thailand, at every turn, it seems that some exploratory fly angler is opening up whole new horizons for our sport in terms of both species and geography. The parochial, old-school view of a non-fly species thankfully doesn't even exist anymore, seemingly replaced by the idea that the more unlikely the species and the harder it is to get to, the more attractive and alluring the challenge. And since challenge and discovery are two of the basic pillars of fly fishing, we are lucky to live in a time where neither mind-set nor geography limits our pursuits.

In this light, a simple glance at a map of the world shows almost limitless opportunities for fly fishers. For example, the entire Canadian Arctic, an incredibly vast, essentially uninhabited wilderness of well over a million square miles, still remains virtually unfished, and from personal experience, I can attest to the fact that there are hundreds if not thousands of pristine rivers and lakes up there, many of which hold populations of sea-run Arctic char that would make your mind swim. While not too many have experienced these spectacular fish, as cited in Robert Behnke's book, *Trout and Salmon of North America*, A. J. McClane once wrote that Arctic char "may be quite literally the strongest fish that swims. It is unquestionably the strongest salmonid." Personally, I have no doubt they are the last great anadromous salmonid and one day soon will be revered by fly anglers in the same way sea trout, steelhead, and Atlantic salmon are now. The Russian Arctic is similarly vast and little known, and in addition to Arctic char, which are circumpolar in distribution, it's hard to imagine that there

aren't at least a few spectacular Atlantic salmon streams east of the Kola that we still don't know about. And as far as Russia is concerned, this is to say nothing of Kamchatka, a salmonid fisher's paradise, where only a handful of its hundreds of rivers are fished.

Similarly, south of the equator, much of the enormous Amazon basin remains truly wild and undiscovered, and while anglers increasingly travel there for giant peacock bass, we've barely scratched the surface, both in terms of region and fish species. One day soon, I know I will see photos of fly anglers from deep within the Brazilian Amazon holding up huge, fly-caught arapaimas, and with any luck, I will be among them. Also, in that part of the world, in my estimation, the spectacular freshwater dorado is still a highly underrated species, and while more and more of us go to fish them near the Esteros del Ibera, in northeastern Argentina, they and other great fish like the pira pita can be found all the way into the little known wilds of Bolivia. The point being, while we often think that there is nothing left on earth to discover, for global fly fishing and wilderness opportunities, it's exactly the opposite.

Closer to home though, the outlook often doesn't seem as bright. In both Canada and the United States, water and wilderness seem to be disappearing before our eyes, and our fish and fishing experiences too often are not even given a passing consideration where commerce and economic growth are perceived to hang in the balance. And, in all too many cases, our elected officials and government agencies entrusted with fisheries management seem to act in such short-sighted and directly contrary ways to not only our interests as fly fishers, but to common sense in general, that, at best, the politics of our fisheries can be frustrating and maddening, and, at worst, downright disheartening.

At the time of this writing, just in British Columbia and Alaska alone, we face two potentially catastrophic environmental travesties. In Alaska, the Pebble Mine project threatens the vitally important Lake Iliamna–Bristol Bay system, home to one of the world's most significant Pacific salmon runs and trout populations. And in British Columbia, proposed coal bed methane extraction in the northwest corner threatens three of the province's major river systems: the Skeena, Nass, and Stikine. In one fell swoop, this project compromises not just the significant salmon runs of this region, but also virtually all of the world's most famous steelhead tributaries for which this area is renowned: the Babine, Sustut, Kispiox, Copper, Bulkley, and Damdochax, to name just a few. These are two of the most frightening proposals in terms of scale and potential environmental damage that I've ever seen in my life as a fly fisher. As expected, though, fly fishers are on the front lines of opposition to both, and we can only hope that our impact is felt and some level of sanity will prevail as the future of these projects is determined.

While issues of this magnitude of course involve far more than the preservation of fly-fishing experiences, I think we have a critically important role to play in their eventual outcome wherever they arise in the world. And while it is true that we represent just a tiny share of the overall angling population, let alone the populance at large, we also exert a disproportionately large impact on conservation issues. In almost all such cases, fly fishers are the proverbial canaries in the coal mine. The very nature of our sport, even more so than other types of angling, is highly sensitive to and dependent on healthy environmental conditions, and we are therefore always among the first to notice and to care about adverse impacts in this regard. Fly fishers are also disproportionately represented in a positive way in contributing to real conservation efforts from the grass roots all the way on up. We are present everywhere from the educational stream-rehabilitation and conservation efforts of thousands of small local clubs on local streams, right through to the multidimensional international collaborations that contribute to responsible resource stewardship in places of the world that most people have never even heard of.

My first direct experience with conservation and fly fishing on this level was in Kamchatka, where at the time, the Wild Salmon Center initiatives included fly fishing as an integral part of actual scientific research projects on steelhead life history. It was eye opening, to say the least, adding an entire new perspective to the fabric of our sport that I previously hadn't really considered or understood. And since then, in my travels

177

around the world, I have witnessed and been encouraged by other stunning such examples. In Mongolia the initiatives of Sweetwater Travel with the Taimen Conservation Fund takes a broad, holistic approach, joining fly fishing, scientific research, and local cultural and spiritual factors into an overall idea and strategy of ensuring healthy streams for taimen. In northern Argentina, while fishing for freshwater dorado, I was introduced to the breathtakingly ambitious projects of Doug and Kris Tompkins' Conservation Land Trust in its efforts to preserve and restore the Ibera Wetlands, an incredibly diverse and important marshland ecosystem twice the size of the Florida Everglades. As with its famous Pumalin Project in Chile, Conservation Land Trust's approach in Argentina—to buy huge areas of ecologically significant lands and ultimately turn them into national parks—recognizes the importance of a multifaceted approach to modern conservation, and the vital role played by sustainable, environmentally sensitive activities like fly fishing.

No matter where in the world we look, it seems to me that just doing what fly fishers do bodes well for the future of our sport and species and the environments that sustain them. Every day, exploratory fly anglers are finding and opening up exciting new angling opportunities the world over, and most often, they are in the most pristine environments left on earth. And everywhere we go we take not only the conservation ethic that is a cornerstone of our sport but also significant

amounts of hard cash. In so many places both at home and abroad, the economic impacts of fly fishing are significant, and indeed represent viable alternatives to often outdated and environmentally destructive industries. In fact, fly fishing for so many reasons may just represent the ideal form of modern, sustainable ecotourism. From the local clubs right through to guides, lodge owners and operators, and the industry itself, it is difficult to find any sector of our sport where a commitment to conservation and responsible resource use is not a foremost priority.

Today, conserving our waters often seems a bewildering, frustrating process, but making an impact doesn't have to be as daunting, difficult, expensive, nor complex as it might sometime sound. Of course the more involvement we undertake in any cause, the better, but in the case of fly fishing, I think the most important and easiest first step we can all take is to just get out and fish more often. And I haven't met a fly fisher anywhere in the world who wouldn't happily agree to do just that. In fact, I believe the worst thing that can happen to our waters, especially those that have the most discouraging prognoses, is to stop fishing them altogether, for at that point, we abandon all hope and truly admit defeat.

A fly fisher on a stream is a formidable force for conservation, even if he or she doesn't realize it. At the most basic level, an angler by his or her mere presence alone can discourage those who would otherwise cause the stream damage by dumping waste, poaching, or performing other mindless forms of vandalism. And on the other end of the spectrum, just as I believe that no fish is safe from the imagination and dogged determination of the modern fly fisher, neither are the forces that threaten to rob us of the waters and fish we cherish, regardless of where on earth they may be found. Perhaps the tendency toward passionate fanaticism that draws us to fly fishing in the first place carries over to other parts of our lives. Whatever the case, I sincerely hope that if nothing else, this book inspires you to go out and fish more often, whether it's halfway around the globe for some exotic, little-known species, or even an hour away from home for a ten-inch trout. For if you do, I know you will also do whatever is in your power to preserve that pleasure for yourself and for those who will follow in the future. You have no choice—that's what fly fishers do. So let's go forth and fish.

ABOUT THE AUTHOR

Roy Tanami is a prominent international outdoor photographer and a contributing editor to *Wild On The Fly*, a leading fly-fishing travel magazine. He also guides steelhead in northern British Columbia, and is a certified FFF fly-casting instructor. He lives in Vancouver, British Columbia.